ELITE SERIES

EDITOR: MARTIN WINDROW

CW00553079

Vietnam Airborne

Text by GORDON ROTTMAN

Colour plates by RON VOLSTAD

OSPREY PUBLISHING LONDON

Published in 1990 by
Osprey Publishing Ltd
59 Grosvenor Street, London, W1X 9DA
© Copyright 1990 Osprey Publishing Ltd

British Library Cataloguing in Publication Data

Rottman, Gordon
    Vietnam airborne.
    1. Military airborne, to 1980
    I. Title II. Volstad, Ron
    623.74'6'09
    ISBN 0-85045-941-9

Artist's Note

Readers may care to note that the original paintings
from which the colour plates in this book were
prepared are available for private sale. All
reproduction copyright whatsoever is retained by the
publisher. All enquiries to be addressed to:

    Ronald B. Volstad
    P.O. Box 2730
    Canmore
    Alberta
    Canada T0L 0M0

The publishers regret that they can enter into no
correspondence upon this matter.

Filmset in Great Britain
Printed through Bookbuilders Ltd, Hong Kong

Acknowledgements
A large number of individuals generously gave of their time
and knowledge and made this book possible. Among those
deserving of special thanks and an 'Airborne All The Way!'
are: Ken Askins, Steve Capps, Ken Conboy, Cpl. Steve
Danaher (Australian SAS), Shaun M. Darragh (II corps
MIKE Force), Mike George (ARVN Abn. Div.), Sgt. John
Hodges (USMC Force Recon.), Chuck V. Luitgaren (1st
Bde., 101st Abn. Div.), John J. Martin (ARVN Abn. Div.),
Nguyên Ngoc Hanh (ARVN Abn. Div.), LTC Gerrell
Plummer (1st Bde., 1st Cav. Div.), 1st Sgt. Ray E. Poynter
(1st Bde., 1st Cav. Div.) Maj. Richard Schultze (III Corps
MIKE Force), Steve Sherman (Special Forces), Cecil B.
Smyth Jr., Martin Windrow, 82nd Abn. Div. Association,
Red Hats Association, and many others. A very special
thanks goes to my wife Enriqueta, whose patience while I
attempted to sort out the many units' stories was unending.

Abbreviations used:

Units

Det	Detachment
Plt	Platoon
Co	Company
Bty	Battery
Trp	Troop
Bn	Battalion
Sdn	Squadron
Bde	Brigade
Gp	Group
Regt	Regiment
Div	Division

Branches/Misc.

Abn	Airborne
Ambl	Airmobile
AO	Area of Operations
Armd	Armored
Arty	Artillery
ARVN	Army of the Republic of Vietnam
ASA	Army Security Agency
Cav	Cavalry
CIDG	Civilian Irregular Defense Gp.
CTZ	Corps Tactical Zone
Engr	Engineer
HHC	Headquarters & Headquarters Co.
HQ	Headquarters
Inf	Infantry
LLDB	*Luc-Luong Dac-Biêt* (Special Forces)
LRRP	Long Range Recon. Patrol
MI	Military Intelligence
MP	Military Police
MSF	Mobile Strike Force
NVA	North Vietnamese Army
Recon	Reconnaissance
SAS	Special Air Service
SF	Special Forces
SFGA	SF Group (Abn)
TAOR	Tactical Area of Responsibility
TF	Task Force
TDND	*Tiêu-Doan Nhuy-Du* (Abn. Bn.)
VC	Viet Cong

Vietnam Airborne

Introduction

Whether thunderously shouted 'Airborne!' or '*Nhay Du!*', the airborne *ésprit de corps* was a key motivating factor for a select brotherhood of units which once fought in an out-of-the-way corner of the world. The airborne mystique which evolved in World War II was no less alive in the airborne infantry and reconnaissance units that fought in the Republic of Vietnam from the 1950s until the 1970s. The American paratroopers brought the airborne inheritance of the proud units that fought in World War II. The sturdy Vietnamese '*bawouans*' inherited their airborne spirit from their French para mentors. And the others—the Australians, New Zealanders, and Thais—each brought their own brand of airborne tradition to the war.

Vietnam was a guerrilla war fought against a highly motivated, ingenious, elusive enemy. With this war came the related frustrations of dealing with a civilian population of sometimes uncertain loyalties, political turmoil, 'rules' of engagement, and privileged sanctuary to which the enemy could retreat at will. It was also a modern conventional war involving massive multi-division and brigade actions by both sides, pitched battles for critical terrain and cities, and high-tempo operations covering vast areas. The political struggle, politically motivated engagement rules, unrealistic goals and concepts pursued by the higher circles of the military and governments, unpopularity of the war at home, and the sheer war-weariness of the combatants made Vietnam one of the most difficult combat environments ever encountered. When conventional units struggled more or less vainly to operate in this environment, or even showed a reluctance to continue the fight, it was not unusual for the airborne to be called on to enter the fray. The airborne's ability to respond and move rapidly by air transport or helicopter, their flexibility in ever-changing tactical situations, their blunt aggressiveness, and the 'All the Way!' attitude inculcated as part of the airborne spirit were what saved the day in many brutal fights in the jungles, swamps, plains, and mountains of Vietnam.

The airborne were not without their own problems. They, too, were battered by the morale problems inherent to the war; endured misuse and political in-fighting; suffered from battlefield defeats; and struggled to maintain their jump qualification and high training standards. This last factor—training and parachute qualifications—was to be an on-going battle for airborne units. Due to the nature of their operations, their aggressiveness often resulting in high losses, and the short in-country tours, there was a constant turnover in paratroop units. The more specialised airborne units—special operations and reconnaissance—had their own difficulties. Though their small size eased their strength demands, their need for high-calibre troops and the subsequent lengthy training requirements caused their own manning problems.

Airborne training itself was partly to blame for the continuing manpower shortages. The three-week course could only be undertaken after initial entry training and the delays of the selection process. A high wash-out and training injury rate further reduced the number of prospective paratroopers (the author's 1968 class began with 950 and graduated 450). Qualified paratroopers were sometimes lost in the replacement pipeline, hundreds of them being assigned to non-airborne units. Specialised units such as Rangers/LRRPs and Pathfinders, not being supported by a dedicated replacement system, had to recruit from scarce qualified personnel in-country. So desperate were some units for paratroopers that they conducted jump training in-country without benefit of

A platoon leader of Co. B, 3rd Bn., 187th Inf., 101st Abn. Div. displays a captured RPD machine gun and RPG-2 rocket launcher on 'Hamburger Hill', 1969. (Chuck Luitgaren)

A 173rd Abn. Bde. 'tunnel rat' returns fire at close range with a tunnel's occupants. Armed with an M1911A1 .45 calibre pistol, he is uniformed in the early model jungle fatigues with shoulder straps.

the elaborate training devices used at Ft. Benning[1], Tan Son Nhut, and at Dong Ba Thin. The one-year tour of duty was also responsible for a constant turnover in experienced paratroopers; and, even though they were in a combat zone, units in Vietnam still had to compete for men with the many other Army airborne units stationed throughout the world[2].

The airborne infantry and their support units were often employed as 'fire brigades'. Based in central locations throughout Vietnam, they were expected to rush to the aid of endangered outposts and remote units, to respond to enemy units discovered in the rugged mountains and swamps, and to answer the call to rout the dug-in enemy from their fortified mountain strongholds and footholds in the cities. These tasks fell principally to the 173rd Airborne Brigade; 1st Brigade, 101st Airborne Division; ARVN Airborne, and Special Forces' MIKE Forces—all the true gypsies of the war, always on the move. Other smaller units were called on to use their special skills for reconnaissance and direct action strikes. Their war was spent painstakingly locating the enemy, and striking him rapidly—or directing others with more clout to hit him. Yet others used their shadowy uncon-

ventional skills in counterinsurgency and other special covert operations[3].

It was the airborne spirit that drove these units and men. Far beyond the 'hazardous' duty pay[4], it was the inherent motivation, the will to do better, to drive oneself harder and further, the brotherhood found in acceptance into the unit or tribe, and the bonding between the lowest private and the commanding general—for all had gone through the same very special rites of passage.

Major US Army Airborne Units

173rd Airborne Brigade (Separate)

The 173rd Airborne Brigade, know officially as the 'Sky Soldiers' and unofficially as 'The Herd', was activated on 26 March 1963 as one of the Army's first separate combined arms brigades under the new organisation structure. Stationed on Okinawa and tasked as the US Army Pacific Command's ready reaction force, it was maintained at a high state of readiness for deployment to any of the region's potential trouble spots. Intended for immediate parachute insertion, it could seize inland airheads or coastal seaports, to be reinforced by the Hawaii-based 25th Inf. Div. or Okinawa-based 3rd Marine Division.

In early 1965 Marine units began establishing enclaves on South Vietnam's northern coast. Located near the coastal cities of Phu Bai, Da Nang, Chu Lai, and Qui Nhon, the enclaves were to serve as secure bases from which combat operations could be mounted. Gen. Westmoreland, developer of the enclave strategy, requested Army representation in the form of the 173rd Abn. Bde. in April 1965. The orders were given, but the Brigade's mission was to be only temporary: the 'Sky Soldiers' were supposed to be replaced by a brigade of the 101st Abn. Div. within a few months. This was never to take place: not only was 'The Herd' the first Army combat formation to be committed to Vietnam, but it was to become the longest serving. The largest of the Army's separate brigades, its structure often fluctuated:

1st Bn. (Abn.) 503rd Inf.[5]	May 63–Aug. 71
2nd Bn. (Abn.) 503rd Inf.	May 63–Aug. 71
3rd Bn. (Abn.) 503rd Inf.	Oct. 67–Aug. 71
4th Bn. (Abn.) 503rd Inf.	June 66–Aug. 71
3rd Bn. (105mm) (Abn.), 319th Arty.	May 63–Aug. 71
Co. D (Anti-tank) (Abn.), 16th Armor[6]	May 63–Aug. 68

[3] The US Special Forces and Rangers/LRRPs are not a subject of this book; their histories will be found in Elite 4, *US Army Special Forces 1952–84* and Elite 13, *US Army Rangers and LRRP Units 1942–87* in this series.

[4] US hazardous duty, or 'jump', pay was $55 for enlisted men, $110 for officers. Outside of Vietnam an individual was required to make at least one jump every three months to receive the pay. In Vietnam it was paid whether the paratrooper jumped or not.

[5] From 1963 US Airborne Infantry Battalions were composed of an HHC and three rifle companies with about 820 troops. In 1966 a combat support company was added using former HHC assets. In 1967 units began forming a fourth rifle company, and all had one by the end of 1968. Battalion strength was now 920.

[6] Co. D, 16th Armor, equipped with M56 90mm Scorpion self-propelled anti-tank guns, provided the assets for the Tuy Hoa Armor Co. (Provisional) employed by the Brigade from April 1968–Nov. 1969.

[1] The Infantry School's Airborne Department was responsible for the Basic Airborne Course, but the 82nd and 101st Abn. Divs. occasionally conducted their own local courses, as did other units in the US and overseas.

[2] Besides the airborne units in Vietnam, in 1968 the US Army had the 82nd Abn. Div., various XVIII Abn. Corps support units, two infantry battalions in Germany and one in Panama, two LRRP companies in Germany and one in the US, two rifle companies in Alaska, six SF groups, and a company in the US and various countries, two each National Guard and Reserve SF groups, and a National Guard brigade, three LRRP companies, plus smaller units.

Trp. E (Armd.) (Abn.), 17th Cav.	May 63–Aug. 71
Co. N (Ranger), 75th Inf. [1]	Feb 69–Aug. 71
173rd Support Bn. (Abn.)	May 63–Aug. 71
173rd Engineer Co. (Abn.)	May 63–July 71
335th Aviation Co. (Airmobile)	Nov 66–Aug. 71
534th Signal Co. (Abn.) [2]	Dec 68–July 71
172nd MI Det.	May 65–Aug. 71
404th ASA Det.	May 65–Aug. 71

Other combat units were attached to the 173rd for substantial periods:

1st Bn., Royal Australian Regt.	May 65–June 66
1st Bn. (Mech), 50th Inf.	May 68–Sep. 69
3rd Bn. (Airmobile), 506th Inf. [3]	Dec. 69–April 70
39th Inf. Plt. (Scout Dog)	July 66–July 71
75th & 76th Inf. Plts. (Tracker Dog)	

The first elements of the Brigade's then two infantry battalions landed at Bien Hoa, north-east of Saigon, on 7 May 1965. Intended as a country-wide reaction force, for almost two months they pulled security duty at Bien Hoa Air Base and Vung Tau port. Reinforced by 1st Bn., Royal Australian Regt., the Brigade was finally collected together; and executed the largest airmobile operation up to that time. Together with the ARVN 3rd and 8th Abn. Bns. and the 18th ARVN Inf. Div.'s 48th Regt., the 'Sky Soldiers' assaulted into the VC-controlled War Zone D on 27 June. A similar incursion into the enemy stronghold was executed the following month. These operations served the Brigade well in preparing it for its future response-force missions, and refined its airmobility capabilities.

It was not long, however, before the 'fire brigade' was to be employed. A major attack on the Duc Co Special Forces Camp led to the defeat of ARVN units called to support it. The 173rd was airlifted to Pleiku on 10 August 1965, and secured a mountain pass permitting their withdrawal. On 6 September the Brigade returned to Bien Hoa. War Zone D was to be the focus of its operations, many conducted with the 1st Inf. Division. The Australian battalion returned home in June 1966 and was replaced by the 4th Bn., 503rd Inf., formed in April at Ft. Campbell, Kentucky. Additional US divisions and brigades continued to arrive in-country through 1966–67, and it was not long before the nature of the war changed. In May 1966 the Brigade was again rushed to Pleiku to act as the II CTZ reaction force when the 1st Bde., 101st Abn. Div. was attached to Task Force 'Oregon' and sent north. Returning to Bien Hoa in June, the 173rd was committed in November to Operation 'Attleboro', a massive multi-division search and destroy operation into Tay Ninh Province's War Zone C. January 1967 saw the Brigade sent back into the 'Iron Triangle' during Operation 'Cedar Falls'.

The largest operation yet conducted, 'Junction City', kicked off on 22 February 1967 when 845 paratroopers of the 2nd Bn., 503rd Inf.; Bty. A, 3rd Bn., 319th Arty.; and elements of the Bde. HHC jumped from 20 Hercules C-130s on to Drop Zone Red outside Katum. The only large-scale US combat jump of the war, it has often been criticised; a helicopter landing was possible, and it was claimed that the jump was executed only for the purpose of crediting the unit with a combat jump. This charge is unfair, as the principal reason for the parachute insertion was the limited number of available helicopters. The use of C-130s to insert the force freed enough helicopters to project another battalion into the area without having to wait for return lifts. Speed was critical since the aim of the operation was to surround a large enemy force. The paratroopers were followed by a huge airmobile operation inserting eight US and Allied battalions.

The entire Brigade was sent north in June 1967, established itself in Kontum, and quickly became enmeshed in a number of rough close-in fights. The Brigade relocated to Tuy Hoa on the coast, little knowing that its previous actions were to pale in comparison with what lay ahead. The 4th Inf. Div.'s Operation 'MacArthur' began on 11 October with 4th Bn., 503rd Inf. attached. The battle for Dak To and the control of the Central Highlands was about to commence. Bitter fighting erupted, and the Brigade was moved to Dak To. The 3rd Bn., 503rd Inf.—formed in April at Ft. Bragg, NC—joined the Brigade during this period. Battling for Special Forces camps and seemingly endless hilltops, both the 173rd Airborne and 4th Inf. Div. struggled against the cream of the NVA. One of the Brigade's most vicious fights was for Hill 875, fortified by the 174th NVA Regt., from 19 to 23 November. The fighting around Dak To lasted to the end of November resulting in the total defeat of the 1st NVA Div.

1965: 173rd Abn. Bde. paratroopers fill canteens from a 20 gallon lister bag. The trooper to the left carries M72 Light Anti-tank Weapons (LAW) bundled in a sleeping bag carrier.

[1] Co. N, 75th Inf. was formed by redesignating the assets of the 74th Inf. Det. (LRP) on 1 Feb. 1969. The 74th Inf. Det. had been attached to the brigade Dec. 1967–Feb. 1969. It in turn replaced the provisional 173rd LRRP formed in 1965.

[2] The 534th Signal co. replaced the 173rd Signal Co. (Provisional) which had served in the brigade July 1967–Dec. 1968.

[3] Assigned to the 101st Abn. Div. (Ambl).

and other enemy units; but the 173rd was decimated in the process.

The Brigade remained in Binh Dinh and Binh Thuan Provinces throughout 1968 and was not engaged in any major battles, though countless small scale operations were conducted during Operation 'McLain' from January 1968 to January 1969. The 'Hawk' concept of small hunter-killer team operations was developed during this time. Squad and platoon-sized ambushes would be established at night by companies throughout an assigned area, with an airmobile reaction force on stand-by. The 3rd Bn., 503rd Inf. was attached from July 1968 to September 1969 to Task Force 'South', a provisional brigade-sized force formed to counter enemy activity in southern II CTZ. The 173rd also became involved in the 'Pair-Off' programme with the 22nd and 23rd ARVN Inf. Divs. as part of the Vietnamisation programme. The longest duration operation conducted by the 173rd was 'Washington Green' from 15 April 1969 to 1 January 1971—the pacification of Binh Dinh Province's An Lao Valley.

'The Herd' departed Vietnam on 25 August 1971. The colours were moved to Ft. Campbell; and the brigade that had been maintained as the Army's one fully airborne qualified unit in Vietnam was inactivated on 14 January 1972. Exemplifying the airborne infantry spirit, the 'Sky Soldiers' were awarded the Presidential Unit Citation (for Dak To), the Meritorious Unit Citation, and Vietnamese Gallantry

A 173rd Abn. Bde. rifle squad struggles through III CTZ swamps, 1967. Full-colour insignia are still in use.

Cross and Civil Action Unit Citations. The 1st and 2nd Bns., 503rd Inf. also received the PUC and the MUC. The 4th Bn., 503rd Inf. and 3rd Bn., 319th Arty. received the MUC.

101st Airborne Division

The only airborne division to be fully combat committed since World War II, the 101st Airborne [1] began its Vietnam service when its 1st Brigade was deployed in the summer of 1965. The 'Eagle Brigade' was ordered to Vietnam as a permanent replacement for the 173rd Airborne. Fully airborne qualified, the Brigade arrived at Cam Ranh Bay on 29 July, establishing its first headquarters at Bien Hoa. Due to the war's escalation the 173rd remained in-country; the 'Eagle Brigade' was now to act as II CTZ's fire brigade, in the same manner as the 173rd in III CTZ.

The Brigade's first operation, the following month, was to open Highway 19 connecting Qui Nhon on the coast with An Khe in the Central Highlands. Operation 'Highland', intended to clear the area for the arrival of the 1st Cav. Div., proved to be a good shakedown exercise for the Brigade. Operation 'Gibraltar' in September was a different matter. This pitted Brigade elements against NVA units for the first time and, while the operation was a success, the 'Screaming Eagles' paid dearly. In December the Brigade established its headquarters at Phan Rang in southern II CTZ, there to remain until May 1967. In early 1966 the 1st Bde. aided the Korean 2nd Marine Bde. and ARVN units in Operation 'Van Buren', the clearing of Phu Yen Province. June saw the 'Eagle Brigade' engaged beside ARVN units in the Kontum area during Operation 'Hawthorne'.

In May 1967 the 1st Bde. was attached to Task Force 'Oregon' [2]. Its headquarters was temporarily moved to Duc Pho, returning to Phan Rang in July. The Task Force and the 'Eagle Brigade' operated in Quang Ngai and Quang Tin Provinces until the TF was replaced by the 23rd Inf. ('Americal') Div. in September. The Brigade continued to operate in southern II CTZ, executing Operation 'Klamath Falls', until moved south with the remainder of the 101st Airborne in January 1968.

One imaginative 1st Bde. initiative was the employment of its three infantry battalion reconnaissance platoons as Recondos [3]. These 20-plus-man platoons were initially equipped for more conventional operations with seven $\frac{1}{4}$-ton utility trucks (jeeps), five mounting M60 machine guns and two with 106mm recoilless rifles. The nature of the war and II CTZ's terrain prevented effective use of this mobility. The platoons turned in their jeeps and trained extensively in reconnaissance and ambush patrols using Recondo techniques. They would patrol assigned areas and, once the enemy was located, airmobile reaction forces supported by artillery and gunships would respond. Each platoon adopted a fitting title: 1st Bn., 327th Inf—'Tiger Force'; 2nd Bn., 327th Inf—

[1] The 101st Abn. Div. was formed on 15 August 1942 as one of the Army's first two airborne divisions. Serving in the European Theatre, the Division was inactivated in late 1945. It was subsequently reactivated three times as a training division in the late 1940s and early 1950s. In May 1954 it was finally reactivated as a full airborne division.

[2] TF 'Oregon' was a provisional division-sized force established to protect the southern portion of I CTZ; permitting the US Marines to concentrate in the north to secure the DMZ from increasing NVA infiltration. Its other brigades were 3rd Bde., 25th Inf. Div. and 196th Inf. Bde. (Light).

[3] 'Recondo' is the acronym for 'RECONnaissance commanDO'. The concept was developed by Maj. Gen. Westmoreland while commanding the 101st Airborne in 1959. Two- and three-week Recondo Courses were conducted by some divisions over the years and were, in effect, 'mini-Ranger' courses.

A 1st Bn., 506th Inf., 101st Abn. Div. sergeant, engaged in Operation 'TODD FOREST' in 1969, rests his load on some 5.56mm ammunition crates and sandbags. His nylon rucksack has been attached to the upper portion of its frame.

3rd Bn., 187th Inf., 101st Abn. Div. paratroopers rest on a shell-battered ridge leading to 'Hamburger Hill', 1969. (Chuck Luitgaren).

'Hawk Recon'; and 2nd Bn., 502nd Inf. — 'Recondos'. Virtually all battalion reconnaissance platoons in Vietnam were eventually to operate in a similar manner.

The remainder of the 101st Abn. Div., back at Ft. Campbell, was initially scheduled to deploy to Vietnam in June 1968. It had not been idle, however: in July 1967 some of its battalions were committed to civil disturbance control in Detroit, Michigan. Gen. Westmoreland feared that the North Vietnamese would agree to freeze committed troop levels in South Vietnam after the planned 1967 holiday cease-fire (they never did); and in early August the 'Screaming Eagles' were alerted for an early departure. The Division was far from ready, however.

Since 1965 one of the Division's principal tasks had been to provide parachute-qualified replacements to its 1st Bde. and the 173rd Airborne; the 82nd Airborne was spared from this drain as it was maintained as a full-strength strategic reserve. The 101st was so drastically understrength that over 6,000 paratroopers were needed; but only non-airborne replace-

ments were drawn from other units. To make matters worse, almost 500 of the Division's scarce paratroopers were pulled out and reassigned to the 173rd Airborne to make good its losses at Dak To. In this state—and for all practical purposes a non-airborne formation—the remainder of the 'Screaming Eagles' began arriving in Vietnam on 18 November 1967. The 2nd Bde. went to Cu Chi, the 3rd to Phoc Vinh, and the Div. HQ to Bien Hoa. The 1st Bde. moved to Song Be in III CTZ in January 1968 where it conducted operations in War Zone D. The Division was composed of:

HHC, 1st Bde., 101st Abn. Div*
    1st Bn. (Abn.), 327th Inf.*
    2nd Bn. (Abn.), 327th Inf.*
    2nd Bn. (Abn.), 502nd Inf.*
    3rd Bn. (Abn.), 506th Inf.
HHC, 3rd Bde., 101st Abn. Div.
    1st Bn. (Abn.), 501st Inf.
    2nd Bn. (Abn.), 501st Inf.
    1st Bn. (Abn.), 502nd Inf.
HHC, 3rd Bde., 101st Abn. Div.
    3rd Bn. (Abn.), 187th Inf.
    1st Bn. (Abn.), 506th Inf.

Hawk Recon. Plt., 2nd Bn., 327th Inf., 101st Abn. Div. operating in I CTZ in August 1970. All wear the camouflage jungle fatigues; in the early days the 1st Bde. recon. platoons wore tiger-strip camouflage. Their unofficial scroll can be seen over the airborne tab.

An excellent view of 1st Cav. Div. radio-telephone operators (RTO) with AN/PRC-25 radios festooned with M18 coloured smoke grenades. Radio equipment accessory bags are attached to the radios' left sides. The bareheaded man is armed with an XM177E2 SMG.

2nd Bn. (Abn.), 506th Inf.
HHB, 101st Abn. Div. Arty.
    2nd Bn. (105mm) (Abn.), 319th Arty.
    2nd Bn. (105mm) (Abn.), 320th Arty. *
    1st Bn. (105mm) (Abn.) 321st Arty.
HHC, 101st Abn. Div. Support Command
    326th Medical Bn. (Abn.)
    426th Supply and Service Bn. (Abn.)
    801st Ordnance Maintenance Bn. (Abn.)
    101st Administrative Co. (Abn.)
    SERTS [1]
Division Troops
    2nd Sdn. (Armd.) (Abn.), 17th Cav.
    101st Aviation Bn. (Abn.)
    326th Engr. Bn. (Combat) (Abn.)
    501st Signal Bn. (Abn.)

101st MP Co. (Abn.)
Attached units
    Co. L (Ranger), 75th Inf. [2]
    101st MI Co.
    265th ASA Co.
    36th Chemical Det.
    42nd Inf. Plt. (Scout Dog)
    557th Inf. Plt. (Tracker Dog)

* These units served with 1st Bde., 101st Abn. Div. when deployed to Vietnam as a separate brigade. Other units comprising 1st Bde. included:

101st Support Bn. (Provisional) (Abn.)
Trp. A, 2nd Sdn. (Armd.) (Abn.), 17th Cav.
Co. A, 326th Engr. Bn. (Combat) (Abn.)
Co. B, 501st Signal Bn. (Abn.)
20th Chemical Det.
181st MI Det.
406th ASA Det.

The Division's first weeks in-country were spent training its hastily assembled troops by conducting operations in

[1] 'Screaming Eagle Replacement Training School.' As with all divisions and separate brigades in Vietnam, the 101st operated a two-week combat orientation and acclimatisation school for newly assigned troops.

[2] Formed from the assets of Co. F (LRP), 58th Inf. on 1 Feb. 1969.

'semi-pacified areas'. The year 1968 was to see few opportunities for the 101st to serve together, its brigades repeatedly being rushed piecemeal to trouble spots. One of its battalions, 3rd Bn., 506th Inf., was attached to a variety of units from July 1968, and was not to serve with its parent division again until September 1970.

In January the 2nd Bde. was shifted to I CTZ to support the 1st Cav. Div. near Hue. In February the Div. HQ and 1st Bde. also moved to the vicinity of Hue to support the Khe Sanh relief operation. The 1st Bde. had driven VC troops from Song Be during a bitter house-to-house fight earlier in the month. In the north they conducted operations in the lowlands of Quang Tri and Thua Thien Provinces throughout May. The 3rd Bde. remained in III CTZ, where it participated in several Tet-68 actions. In late May the 3rd Bde. was 'secretly' moved to Kontum in an effort to deceive the NVA over the Division's future operations. This achieved no reaction on the enemy's part however, and the 3rd returned to Phouc Vinh the next month. In mid-August much of the 101st was deployed to the A Shau Valley for Operation 'Somerset Plain'. Employing airmobile tactics, the Division soon drove the NVA from their valley base area into neighbouring Laos, but the enemy would quickly reoccupy the critical valley when the Americans departed. This time they dug in to await the 101st Airborne's return. In early September the 3rd Bde., now back in III CTZ, became involved in a rough battle at Trang Bang. In October the Division was finally collected in various locations in III CTZ. This was to be short-lived, as December found the Division's units back in northern I CTZ.

In February 1969 the Division established two fire support bases on the edge of the A Shau Valley in response to intelligence reports of a massive NVA build-up. Operation 'Massachusetts Striker' began on 1 March with 2nd Bde. airmobiling four battalions into the valley. This operation was to last through May, when 3rd Bde. kicked off Operation 'Apache Snow', the largest incursion yet into the A Shau. On 10 May the battle for Ap Bia Mountain, or Hill 937, began; it was soon to become known as 'Hamburger Hill'. Three 101st battalions and an ARVN battalion fought bitterly for the hill mass, finally securing it on 20 May after suffering terrible losses.

In January 1968 US Army, Vietnam conducted a study on the future availability of paratroopers. Due to the drain of combat losses (paratroopers are generally aggressive fighters and tend to suffer high casualties), the limitations of the one-year duty tour, and the demands of competing for qualified jumpers with the 82nd Airborne and Special Forces, it was determined that it would be difficult to maintain even the 173rd Airborne on jump status. It was decided to convert the 101st into an airmobile division like the 1st Cavalry. This process was begun in July 1969. The last 1st Bde. battalions were taken off jump status on 26 August 1969.

The 101st was to remain in Vietnam until it began return-

A 1st Cav. Div. platoon leader directs his men to a new location. He is carrying a nylon rucksack with a two-quart canteen attached to the top. Most of the soldiers are carrying their M16 magazines in bandoliers rather than ammo pouches.

1st Bde., 1st Cav. Div. officers confer with a 40th ARVN Inf. Regt. advisor (centre): Bong Son, 1966. The officer on the right wears a Ranger tab over the 1st Cav. Div. patch (Gerrell Plummer)

ing home in December 1971, with the last elements departing in February 1972. The 'Screaming Eagles' returned to their traditional home at Ft. Campbell where they remain to this day as the Army's only air assault division. The 1st and 3rd Bdes. were awarded the Presidential Unit Citation and Valorous Unit Award, with most other divisional units receiving similar US and Vietnamese awards.

1st Brigade (Airborne), 1st Cavalry Division (Airmobile)

On 1 July 1965 at Ft. Benning, Georgia, the 1st Cav. Div.[1] was converted into the Army's first airmobile combat division. The raising of this division is an unusual story in itself. The airmobile concept had its origins with the 1962 Howze Board, a study to determine the feasibility of further developing the helicopter as a means of battlefield tactical mobility. This led to the creation of the 11th Air Assault Div.

(TEST)[2] at Ft. Benning on 15 February 1963. Its purpose was to test the concepts, operational techniques, aircraft, and equipment for an airmobile division. The 11th was far from a full strength formation, having only one brigade of infantry. For multi-brigade exercises additional battalions were borrowed from the 2nd Inf. Div.. On 1 October 1963 selected divisional units were made airborne:

1st Bn. (Abn./Ambl.), 187th Inf.
Bty. B (Abn.), 6th Bn. (105mm) (Ambl.), 81st Arty.
Co. A (Abn.), 127th Engr. Bn. (Combat) (Ambl.)
11th Aviation Pathfinder Co. (Provisional)[3]
165th Aerial Equipment Support Det. (Abn)[3]

The tests were highly successful, and a decision was made to include a full airmobile division in the force structure. There was a certain amount of opposition to the creation of an airmobile division, some feeling that it would tie up a disproportionate number of helicopters dedicated to a single formation, and others urging more testing and exercises before the fielding of such an extravagant force. However, while all this debate was taking place the situation was rapidly deteri-

[1] The 1st Cav. Div. was activated on 13 September 1921 at Ft. Bliss, Texas. It served on the Mexican border until February 1943 when it was dismounted and reorganised and redesignated 1st Cav. Div., Special in December. It fought in the Pacific and was part of the Army of Occupation in Japan. In 1950–53 it saw action in Korea, remaining there after the cease-fire.

[2] The 11th Abn. Div. was originally activated on 25 February 1943 at Camp Mackall, NC, subsequently serving in the Pacific Theatre and with the Army of Occupation in Japan. It returned to the US in May 1949 and was stationed at Ft. Campbell, Kentucky. In April 1956 the 'Angels' were moved to Germany and inactivated on 1 July 1958.

[3] These units were added at a later date.

orating in Vietnam's Central Highlands—a vast region with varied terrain and changeable weather conditions. Supporters of the airmobile concept felt that this was an ideal situation to prove the division's value, and it was recommended that it be deployed as soon as possible.

The 11th itself had been intended only as a test unit. The new division was to be designated the 1st Cavalry Division (Airmobile), known as the 'First Team' to its troopers. However, the 1st Cavalry, organised as a standard infantry division, was stationed in Korea at the time. The colours of the 1st Cav. and 2nd Inf. Divs. were exchanged, and the new airmobile division was formed on 15 July 1965 using the assets of the 11th Air Assault and 2nd Inf. Divs., 10th Transportation Bde. (Air Transport)—providing some of the helicopters and fixed-wing aircraft—and smaller aviation units drawn from throughout the Army.

The division was given a mere three months to prepare for deployment and combat. When formed it had less than 9,500 of the required 15,787 troops, and lacked a great deal of specialised equipment. Some units even had to be formed from the ground up.

The 1st Cavalry was authorised 438 helicopters and light fixed-wing aircraft, as opposed to 101 in a standard infantry division. One-third of its combat and combat support elements could be moved by organic helicopters in a single lift. This gave the division a unique high-speed battlefield mobility and an unprecedented tactical flexibility. Not all of the helicopters were for troop transport; the unit possessed substantial airborne firepower in the form of machine gun and rocket-armed helicopter gunships.

Three of the division's eight airmobile infantry battalions were to be airborne qualified, on the insistence of its commander, Maj. Gen. Harry W. O. Kinnard, a long-time airborne advocate. Comprising the 1st Bde. (Abn.)[1], the battalions were formed by redesignating the three original 11th Div. airmobile infantry battalions. With fewer than 900 qualified jumpers assigned, volunteers were rushed through shortened jump courses to provide the required 3,470 paratroopers. The airborne units included:

1st Bn. (Abn./Ambl.), 8th Cav.[2]
2nd Bn. (Abn./Ambl.), 8th Cav.
1st Bn. (Abn./Ambl.), 12th Cav.
2nd Bn. (105mm) (Abn./Ambl.), 19th Arty.
Co. A (Abn.), 8th Engr. Bn. (Combat) (Ambl.)
1st Cav. Div. Pathfinder Co. (Provisional)
Aerial Equipment & Support Co. (Abn.), 15th Supply & Service Bn.
Co. A (Abn), 15th Medical Bn.
Det. A (Abn), 27th Maint. Bn.

Preparations to meet the deadline for deployment to Vietnam were frantic. A 1,000-man advanced detachment was airlifted to Vietnam and established a base camp near the An Khe Special Forces camp at the end of August 1965.

The base's initial security was provided by 1st Bde., 101st Abn. Division. The bulk of the division was shipped by sea transport, with the 1st Bde. aboard the USNA *Geiger*; disembarking at Qui Nhon on 12 September. The 'First Team' was the first complete US Army division to deploy to Vietnam. Each of the brigades were assigned a TAOR, with the 1st being given Pleiku Province in the heart of the Central Highlands. Units were to see combat just over three months after the new division's formation. In October 1965 the NVA had commenced a major operation with the aim of cutting South Vietnam in half through the Central Highlands. The 1st Brigade's first operation designated was 'All The Way', after the Brigade's—and the airborne's—motto. This was an airmobile operation in late October in support of an ARVN relief column fighting its way to the besieged Plei Me Special Forces camp.

The 1st Bde. was then given the mission of locating enemy units withdrawing through the Ia Drang Valley to Cambodia. The Brigade, in conjunction with 1st Sdn., 9th Air Cav., developed the opening stages of the vicious battle for the Ia Drang until replaced by the 3rd Bde. in November. The 1st Bde. had made good use of the division's massive airmobility assets to locate and fix the enemy.

The Ia Drang had taken its toll of the Division as a whole: combat losses and tropical diseases had cost the 1st Cav. over 25 per cent of its troops. Replacements were quickly assigned,

The XO of Co. B, 1st Bn., 8th Cav., 1st Cav. Div. examines a shattered M16 belonging to one of his company's KIAs: Bong Son, 1966. (Gerrell Plummer)

[1] The 1st Cav. Bde. was originally formed on 29 August 1917 as part of the 15th Cav. Div. and transferred to the new 1st Cav. Div. in 1921. The two-brigade structure was retained until 25 March 1949, though relinquished by the rest of the Army in 1942. From 20 May 1949 to 24 Nov. 1950 the Brigade served in Germany as the 1st Constabulary Bde. The brigade structure was re-established within the Army in 1963 and the 1st Bde., 1st Cav. Div. reactivated on 1 Sept.

[2] The 1st Cavalry's infantry battalions carried cavalry regiment lineages; so designated for traditional reasons and they organised the same as airborne battalions.

but this drastically affected the Division's level of training. This deficiency was doubled for the 1st Bde., as few of its replacements were airborne qualified. Hasty unit-run jump courses were conducted, with the new jumpers making their qualifying jumps from helicopters. Airborne qualification was to be a continuing problem, as it was for all airborne units in Vietnam.

The beginning of 1966 saw the 1st Cavalry focusing·on the II CTZ's coastal region. Late January saw the beginning of a year-long offensive against NVA/VC forces in the coastal Binh Dinh Province. A long succession of operations, beginning with 'Masher/White Wing' lasting from late January to early March, made extensive use of the Division's helicopters and brought many refinements to their employment. These operations often consisted of relentless airmobile pursuits of enemy units through the Bong Son Plains and mountain valleys, followed by bitter firefights on the jungled slopes between inserted cavalrymen and the elusive enemy. In March 1966 the 1st Bde. returned to the Ia Drang during the highly successful Operation 'Lincoln'.

An RTO of Co. B, 2nd Bn., 8th Cav., 1st Cav. Div. tries out an NVA bugle in the Ia Drang Valley.

Operation 'Crazy Horse' was initiated by a 1st Bde. contact in mid-May while providing area security for a newly constructed Special Forces camp. Lasting until June, 'Crazy Horse' was successful in thwarting NVA plans to destroy the new camp. This was followed by Operations 'Nathan Hale' and 'Henry Clay' in the Tuy Hoa area.

In September 1966 the Division executed its largest airmobile operation to date as part of Operation 'Thayer I'. Both the 1st and 2nd Bdes. were inserted in an NVA-infested area known as the 'Crow's Foot'. Most of the NVA managed to slip away, but the operation succeeded in disrupting the enemy's activities in the region and uncovered several large supply caches and support facilities. 'Thayer I' was followed by Operation 'Irving', a more successful effort to dislodge the NVA dug in on coastal hill masses. What followed is still a classic example of airmobile tactics, employed by the 1st Brigade. Air cavalry scout units pinpointed the enemy positions. These were pinned by helicopter gunships and ground scouts. Airmobile rifle companies were rapidly inserted, and the Cavalry's 'Skytroopers' closed with the dug-in NVA, supported by artillery helicoptered to the battlefield. As the surviving enemy attempted to withdraw through monsoon-flooded valleys, the 'Skytroopers' exploited the situation by

inserting companies in front of the struggling NVA during the follow-on Operation 'Thayer II'.

It was during 1966 that the struggle to maintain the 1st Brigade's airborne qualification was all but given up. Competing with the 173rd Abn. Bde., 82nd and 101st Abn. Divs., Special Forces, and the many other airborne units deployed across the world, the 1st Cavalry found it impossible to maintain a viable parachute capability. More experienced paratroopers, already sadly reduced by combat, were lost when their one year tour of duty ended. The massive helicopter assets available had also precluded the need for parachute insertion. In November 1966 the decision was made to terminate the 1st Brigade's airborne status by discontinuing the few remaining paratroopers' jump pay. The Brigade's airborne *ésprit de corps* had served the Division well in the difficult early days of deployment, but had been replaced within the 'First Team' as a whole by a new airmobile spirit, making the 1st Cav. one of the most highly motivated and effective divisions in the war.

The 1st Cavalry and its 1st Bde. were to remain in Vietnam until April 1971. During the period that the 1st Bde. was airborne it earned the Presidential Unit Citation and the Vietnamese Gallantry Cross. Both 1st and 2nd Bns., 8th Cav. and 1st Bn., 19th Arty also earned the PUC for the Pleiku campaign and the 1st Bn. (less Co. A) earned a second one during Operation 'Crazy Horse'. The 1st Bn., 12th Cav. received the PUC during Operation 'Irving'.

3rd Brigade, 82nd Airborne Division

The NVA/VC Tet Offensive whirlwind tore through Vietnam on 25 January 1968. Free World forces fought

Troops of Co. C, 2nd Bn., 8th Cav., 1st Cav. Div. unload a UH-1H during the battle of Dak To.

bitter defensive battles for every major town and military base. Gradually they went over to the offensive as enemy units spent their momentum battering themselves against devastating firepower. Caught unawares, and stunned by the extent of the country-wide offensive, Gen. Westmoreland called for immediate reinforcements. The Ft. Bragg-based 82nd Abn. Div.[1] was one of the few combat-ready units remaining in the US. Other units were at reduced strength and equally lowered readiness due to the equipment drain demanded by Vietnam, and limited training funds. The Army, even in light of the immediate crisis in Vietnam, was reluctant to commit its principal strategic reserve force. Besides its worldwide reaction force rôle, the 'All Americans' were needed at home. Anti-war protests and racial disturbances were breaking out across the country and the 82nd along with other Regular Army units, were needed to augment the hard-pressed National Guard. Divisional battalions were used to quell riots in Detroit in July 1967, and both the 1st and 2nd Bdes. were to be committed to the Washington, DC riots in April 1968.

The situation was desperate enough in Vietnam, however, that the decision was made to immediately deploy the

[1] The 82nd Div. had been activated in 1917 and served in Europe during World War I. After the war it served as a reserve unit until 1942 when it was ordered to active duty. It was reorganised as an airborne division on 15 Aug. 1942 at Camp Claiborne, Louisiana. Serving in the European Theatre in World War II, it returned to Ft. Bragg, NC, where it has remained ever since.

A rigger of the Aerial Equipment and Support Co., 15th Supply and Service Bn., 1st Cav. Div., wearing the traditional red baseball cap, prepares a load of 105mm ammo for helicopter sling loading. Riggers had three principal duties: parachute packing, parachute repair, and preparation of equipment and supplies for airdrop and air movement.

Division's 3rd Brigade[1]. Alerted in the first days of February, other division units had to be stripped of paratrooper-qualified NCOs and troopers to bring the 3rd Bde. up to strength. Even the Special Forces Training Group was looted in a frantic effort to find qualified troops. The advance party was on its way on the 14th. Within days the entire 3,650-man 'Golden Brigade' was flown into Chu Lai by 140 airlift sorties. In the hurry to deploy the Brigade, individual eligibility for combat and overseas deployment was ignored. Once on the ground it was found that few of the troops met the criteria, many only having recently returned from a gruelling Vietnam tour or other lengthy overseas assignment. Given the choice, over 2,500 paratroopers took the option to return to Ft. Bragg. Their replacements were drawn from replacement pools in Vietnam, troops originally destined for and sorely needed by other units. Filled with mostly 'straight leg' replacements, what had been a fully qualified airborne brigade was soon turned into just another light infantry brigade. The 3rd Bde. was augmented with additional units, some after its arrival in-country, enabling it to operate as a separate brigade:

1st Bn. (Abn.), 505th Inf.
2nd Bn. (Abn.), 505th Inf.
1st Bn. (Abn.), 508th Inf.
2nd Bn. (105mm) (Abn.), 321st Arty.
Trp. B, 1st Sdn. (Armd.) (Abn.), 17th Cav.
Co. C, 307th Engr. Bn. (Combat) (Abn.)
58th Signal Co. (Forward Area Support)
82nd Support Bn. (Abn.)
Co. A, 82nd Aviation Bn. (Abn.)
Co. O (Ranger), 75th Inf.

[1] The 3rd Bde., 82nd Abn. Div. was activated on 6 March 1964; it carries the lineage of the World War I 156th Inf. Bde., 78th Div. and the World War II 78th Recon. Co.

A gun crew of the 1st Bn., 21st Arty. prepare to fire an M102 105mm howitzer. This was the standard artillery piece used by all airborne and airmobile units.

52nd Chemical Det.
408th ASA Det.
518th MI Det.
37th Inf. Plt. (Scout Dog)
3rd Plt., 82nd MP Co. (Abn.)

The Brigade was quickly deployed to I CTZ and based outside Phu Bai with the mission of protecting the southern approaches to Hue, which was still the scene of bitter fighting. This all too brief period allowed the Brigade to achieve some semblance of organisation, to acclimatise, and undergo minimal unit re-training. On 9 March they were attached to their traditional arch-rivals, the 101st Abn. Div. (Airmobile). The Brigade's first action was on 11 March when elements responded to a convoy ambush. With the 101st they participated in Operation 'Carentan' where they initiated hunter-killer patrols against infiltrating VC units. This was followed by 'Carentan II' from 1 April to mid-May, in conjunction with the 101st Abn. and 1st ARVN Inf. Divisions. Both operations took place in Quang Tri and Thua Thien Provinces. On 1 May 1968 the 3rd Bde. was

3rd Bde., 82nd Abn. Div. soldiers during an awards ceremony, 1970. All insignia are subdued with the exception of the full-colour 82nd patch. Name and US Army tapes are correctly being worn 'straight', as required in late 1969, as opposed to parallel with the top of the pocket as previously required. Note that none wear jumpwings, since few of the Brigade were airborne-qualified after its initial deployment. The airborne tab was authorised for wear by non-airborne individuals as it designated the unit rather than the man.

placed directly under the command of US Army Vietnam. Continuing security patrols in the Hue–Phu Bai area, the Brigade was not moved until September.

Enemy forces were again threatening Saigon, and the Brigade was moved to this area where they executed aggressive patrols to protect Tan Son Nhut Air Base and north-west Saigon from rocket attack. Placed under the Capitol Military Assistance Command, they also undertook a civic action campaign, providing aid to civilians in the war-torn surrounding countryside. The Brigade's effectiveness can be demonstrated by the fact that no enemy rockets were launched into Saigon from its TAOR. It was during this period that Brigade units were often attached to the 1st Cav. and 25th Inf. Divs., with whom they participated in operations throughout III CTZ. The Brigade was later moved to Phu Loi, west of Saigon, and continued its security mission. From May 1969 combined operations were being conducted with the ARVN Abn. Div. and Ranger Command in preparation for their assuming total responsibility for Saigon's security.

This took place in September, the Brigade being notified at the same time that they would return to the US in December. The Brigade's final major operation in Vietnam began that same month. During Operation 'Yorktown Victor' combat patrols were thrust into the enemy-controlled 'Iron Triangle' north of Saigon. In mid-October the Brigade's battalions, one at a time, began standing down for redeployment preparations. On 11 December 1969 the 3rd Bde. returned to Ft. Bragg. All of its major equipment was turned over in-country for eventual issue to ARVN units. On 15 December, the 4th Bde., raised on 3 July 1968 to bring the 82nd to near full strength, was inactivated.

The 3rd Bde. as a whole was awarded the Vietnamese Gallantry Cross. Numerous subordinate units received awards ranging from the Presidential Unit Citation, Valorous Unit Award and Meritorious Unit Commendation, to various Vietnamese citations.

Other US Airborne Units

Pathfinders
The US Army's Pathfinders had their origins during World War II. The concept, pioneered by the British, was first employed by the 82nd Abn. Division's 505th Parachute Inf. Regt. during the Sicily landings in July 1943, although the 509th PIR had tested it earlier in the year in North Africa. The 82nd then formed an experimental Pathfinder group in Italy in October 1943. The original concept was for specially trained paratroopers to jump in prior to the main force's arrival to pinpoint and mark parachute drop and glider landing zones. This was accomplished by the use of radar homing devices, lights, marker panels, and smoke. The Pathfinder concept was adopted by all airborne divisions and used in all subsequent airborne operations with varying success. A Pathfinder School was established in England in 1944 and moved to Ft. Benning in 1946.

The Pathfinder rôle of guiding transport aircraft was turned over to the Air Force's Combat Control Teams in

1951. They maintained that only qualified Air Force personnel should direct Air Force transports during joint airborne operations. With no further need for Pathfinders, the Ft. Benning school was closed. The increased use of helicopters during the Korean War and the subsequent expansion of Army aviation soon led to new a need for Pathfinders. The Airborne-Army Aviation (later Airborne-Airmobility) Department at Ft. Benning re-established the Pathfinder Course in 1955.

The five-week course taught all aspects of the Pathfinders' new rôle: to select and establish drop and landing zones (helicopter and Army fixed-wing); to establish and operate day and night visual and electronic navigation aids; to furnish ground-to-air communications to provide combat area air traffic control, guidance and ground tactical situation information to Army aircraft; to assist with the assembly of air-delivered troops, supplies and equipment; to provide technical assistance on rigging and sling-loading equipment for air movement; and to aid the co-ordination for on-loading troops, supplies and equipment on aircraft. Pathfinder students, all of whom were airborne-qualified infantrymen, were selected for their leadership abilities and flexibility, since they had to deal directly with aircrews by radio under rapidly changing situations.

The formation of the 11th Air Assault Div. (TEST) in 1963 forced the realisation that with such extensive use of helicopters there was a real need for Pathfinder skills. The 11th Air Assault subsequently formed the 11th Aviation Pathfinder Co. to control all such assets. Teams were attached to aviation and combat units as needed to support airmobile operations. The 1st Cav. Division's deployment to

Marine Gunnery Sgt. Gordon Hopkins and Sgt. Thomas Nicholson, 3rd Force Reconnaissance, December 1966; they pose for a publicity shot with a handful of 'aces of spades' before going out on a mission. (USMC)

Vietnam further served to drive this point home to many critics. As more combat units and aviation battalions were sent to Vietnam the need for Pathfinders increased—far more of them than Ft. Benning was able to provide.

Pathfinder organisation was extremely flexible, with the basic element being the four-man Pathfinder Team. Three or more teams, depending on the size or mission of the supported aviation unit, comprised a Pathfinder Detachment, officially designated, e.g. 5th Infantry Detachment (Pathfinder). Detachments were attached to aviation units on an as-needed basis, and though they had their own numerical designation, were usually known by that of their parent aviation battalion or group. In 1963, prior to the commitment of major combat units to Vietnam, there were only two such detachments. By 1972, when the US withdrew from Vietnam, there were 30 detachments, 26 of which served in Vietnam, along with various provisional teams, sections, detachments, and platoons. On 11 September 1965 the 1st Cav. Div. concentrated its assets in the 1st Cav. Div. Pathfinder Co. under the 11th Aviation Group[1].

Each divisional combat aviation battalion and non-divisional battalions with a troop-lift capability (all assigned to 1st Aviation Bde. after May 1966) had an attached Pathfinder Detachment. They were generally authorised 16 men

[1] Occasionally referred to as 11th Pathfinder Co. (Provisional).

in three four-man Pathfinder Teams and a four-man HQ (also capable of functioning as a team). It was not unusual for these detachments to be unmanned or at greatly reduced strengths. The units' strength and meaningful employment often depended on the parent unit commander's emphasis. Many aviation units felt little need for the Pathfinders' terminal guidance services. Infantry units, too, had little use for Pathfinders as their own proficiency with airmobility operations increased. In reality infantry, artillery, aviation and combat support units became so proficient, and airmobile operations so routine, that all units were capable of performing most Pathfinder missions themselves.

Manning problems also plagued the Pathfinders. It was not uncommon for rifle companies to field only 50 per cent of their authorised strength, and commanders could ill afford to funnel scarce infantrymen to such 'luxury' units as the Pathfinders. Some detachments were manned with non-airborne qualified personnel, and others with paratroopers transferred out of airborne infantry units for 'various reasons'. Many were not Pathfinder qualified, but learned their skills through on-the-job training.

Many units did find the Pathfinders to be of value, and made good use of their skills. Combat area air traffic control at fire support bases was one of the most common. It was not unusual for three or four Pathfinders, commanded by a Spec. 4 and equipped with a single radio, to set up a 'control centre' on some ammo crates and, amid whirlwind clouds of rotor-driven dust, direct hundreds of helicopter arrivals and departures in a single day as a fire support base was estab-

February 1967: two Marine NCOs of 3rd Force Reconnaissance call in air support during an operation near the Laotian border south of the DMZ. (USMC)

lished. They rappelled in and cleared landing zones with explosives, chainsaws, and machetes; secured downed helicopters and rigged them for helicopter extraction; guided Air Force transports during re-supply airdrops; reconnoitered and secured helicopter landing zones; and directed artillery and helicopter gunship fire support.

Though often misused or under-employed—a common occurrence in the US Army for small, specialised units—the Pathfinders in Vietnam performed a valuable and much-needed service in a combat environment so dependent on the helicopter for transport, fire support, and re-supply.

Marine Force Reconnaissance

The US Marine airborne contribution in Vietnam was small, but offered a valuable intelligence-collection capability if properly employed to achieve its maximum effectiveness. Two Force Reconnaissance companies were deployed to Vietnam to provide a deep reconnaissance capability to III Marine Amphibious Force (III MAF), equivalent to a corps-level command. Force Recon. companies are basically LRRP units with a heavy emphasis on amphibious-related skills. They originally had a Pathfinder platoon to establish and operate helicopter landing zones, but this capability was transferred to divisional recon. battalions in 1963. Force Recon. must not be confused with the Marine division recon. battalions, bearing the same designations, but tasked with more conventional reconnaissance missions[1].

Force Recon. Marines are all volunteers, selected on the

[1] Due to the two Companies' designations, 1st and 3rd, it is often assumed they were subordinate to the 1st and 3rd Marine Divisions' recon. battalions, themselves in Vietnam and designated by the same numbers. Although sometimes attached to these divisions, the Force Recon. companies were *force* (corps) units: the fact that they bore the same designations is a coincidence of Marine unit designation practices.

basis of physical endurance and attitude. All personnel are airborne qualified (the recon. battalions are not) at the Army's Ft. Benning jump school, and extensively trained in advanced intelligence collectiom. surveillance, long-range communications, small-boat handling, combat swimming, climbing, survival, and deep evasion and escape skills. These skills were taught in the unit—no Force Recon. course existed at the time. Many are scuba trained by the Navy to accomplish on e of their principal missions, beach reconnaissance in advance of an amphibious landing; this concept was developed by Co. B, 5tgh Recon. Bn. following World War II. Individual training standards are tough even by Marine Corps standards, and some of the corps' best NCOs have served in Force Recon.

The 1st Force Recon. Co. traces its origins to the Headquarters and Service Co., 1st Provisional Amphibious Recon. Bn. activated at Camp Pendleton, California on 11 January 1954, redesignated the Headquarters Section on 31 August. The Battalion was disbanded on 24 February 1955, and elements were formed into the 1st Amphibious Recon. Co. carrying the lineage of the 1st Battalion's Headquarters Section. On 19 January 1957 it was redesignated 1st Force Recon. Co. The unit took part in major exercises in California, Washington, Hawaii, and the Philippines. A Force Recon. company was composed of approximately 180 marines organised into a headquarters platoon and three operations platoons, each with eight four-man teams: team leader, radioman, and two scouts.

In the summer of 1965 the Company was alerted for deployment to Vietnam and shipped to Okinawa in August. From Camp Hague small detachments deployed to Vietnam and the entire company was in-country and based at Da Nang by 24 October. It was relocated to Dong Ha early the following year.

Initially the Company's primary mission was to execute team-sized long range reconnaissance and surveillance patrols to detect enemy infiltration. The standard team is four men, but in Vietnam their size was tailored to each mission and could be larger. The Force Recon. mission began to change in 1966 when conventionally minded Marine officers failed to realise the value of deep penetration intelligence collection, and the extensive pre-infiltration preparations needed to accomplish such missions. The Recon. Marines were directed to begin engaging enemy forces, a mission for which they were not trained or armed, which would compromise their mission, and which would negate their value as a covert intelligence-collection element. On occasion, teams were even marched to base camp perimeters and told to 'just go out and patrol'.

Though grossly misused, and sometimes experiencing the frustration of higher headquarters refusing to believe their reports, both companies still accomplished deep-reconnaissance missions. One such instance came about in the summer of 1966 when 1st Company teams reported large numbers of NVA troops infiltrating across the Demilitarised Zone. At first III MAF was reluctant to accept the reports, but an NVA deserter provided confirmation, and this led to the launching of Operations 'Hastings' and 'Prairie'.

The first Marine combat jump ever executed (no Paramarine units jumped in World War II) was made on 14 June

Marines of 1st Force Reconnaissance board an OV-10 Bronco of Marine Observation Squadron 2 prior to making a non-tactical jump near Da Nang. (USMC)

ARVN paratroopers assault a Hue Citadel palace during Tet-68. Most wear M65 field jackets and M69 body armour vests. The man in the right foreground wears a locally made rain jacket with an integral pack and M16 magazine pockets. (Nguyên Ngoc Hanh)

1966. A hand-picked 13-man team was parachuted from a 1st Marine Aircraft Wing C-1A transport near the tri-border area of Vietnam, Cambodia and Laos, where they ambushed personnel moving supplies. In November 1966 the 1st Company was returned to Da Nang and placed under the control of 1st Recon. Bn. to support Task Force 'X-Ray' at Bhu Bai from January 1967 until September 1968. Their principal task was to emplace remote sensors capable of detecting and electronically reporting the movement of enemy troops. Another jump was made from helicopters on 5 September 1967 by ten Recon. Marines: the mission was a disaster, the small force taking two days to assemble and the team's Navy Corpsman apparently defecting to the NVA. In late 1968 the 1st Company returned to Da Nang and conducted patrol operations in central I CTZ. A final jump was made on 17 November 1969 when the six-man Team 51 parachuted near Nui Tran to conduct a patrol. There is a possibility that other jumps were made, but no records have been found.

The 3rd Force Recon. Co. was activated on 1 November 1965 at Camp Lejeune, NC, to provide Fleet Marine Force, Atlantic with a Force Recon. unit. It moved to Camp Pendleton on 1 September 1966 and began training for Vietnam duty. Arriving at Da Nang in April 1967, it set up camp at Phu Bai, remaining there until moved to Dong Ha on 20 May. It was relocated to Quang Tri Combat Base in January 1969, and then back to Phu Bai on 22 October, remaining there until its departure from Vietnam. The 3rd Company conducted basically the same types of operations as the 1st Company, but made no combat jumps so far as records indicate.

Besides problems of misuse, which became extremely severe by 1969, both units were plagued with training and replacement problems—it takes two years to fully qualify a Force Recon. Marine. The 2nd Force Recon. Co. was raised at Camp Pendleton to replace the 1st Company and support Fleet Marine Force, Pacific, but was soon turned into a training and replacement unit for the 1st and 3rd Companies. Nevertheless, individual training skills deteriorated over the years, and this adversely affected both companies in Vietnam.

In mid-1970 III MAF was about to release both Force Recon. companies to the 1st and 3rd Recon. Bns., again placing them under division control and condemning them to further misemployment. However, before this took place both units were returned to the US. The 1st Company began to stand down in August, departing Vietnam on the 24th; it was subsequently stationed at Camp Pendleton and attached to the 5th Marine Amphibious Brigade. The 3rd Company had begun to stand down in July, departing on 1 August; it was de-activated at Camp Pendleton on the 27th.

Allied Airborne Units

ARVN paratroopers, with their gear carried in poncho rolls, celebrate the flag-raising over Hue's Citadel after its recapture during Tet-68. (Nguyên Ngoc Hanh)

ARVN Airborne

The paratroopers of the Army of the Republic of Vietnam owe their origin and traditions to the French parachute forces of the Indochina War; even after years of American assistance the distinctive French influence could still be seen.

The first Vietnamese paratroop unit was 1st Co. Indochinese Parachutists (*1ere Compagnie Indochinoise Parachutiste—1e CIP*) formed on 1 January 1948 and attached to the French 1st Colonial Commando Parachute Battalion. It made the first of many combat jumps in April with that unit. The 3e, 5e and 7e CIPs soon followed, along with later companies. These companies were attached to French battalions as the fourth company in Metropolitan Parachute Chasseurs Regiments (RCPs, actually battalions) and Foreign Legion Parachute Battalions (BEPs), and as the third and fourth companies in the Colonial Commando Parachute Battalions (BCCPs) which were redesignated Colonial Parachute Battalions—BCPs—in March 1951. When these battalions rotated back to France, the Vietnamese CIPs were re-assigned to their replacement units. The officers and senior NCOs of the CIPs were largely French and provided by the parent battalion. An independent unit, 1st Parachute Guard Co. of North Vietnam (1 CPGNV), was formed in 1949. A Vietnamese National Army was raised by the French in 1949, at least on paper, though Vietnamese units continued to simply augment the French Expeditionary Corps.

The next stage in the evolution of the Vietnamese airborne came on 15 July 1951 when 1 CIP and 1 CPGNV were consolidated in Saigon to form the 1st Bn. of Vietnamese Parachutists (*1er Bataillon de Parachutistes Vietnamiens*—1er BPVN). The French paras gave them the slang name of *bawouans*, the French acronym for BPVN. Jump and unit training were conducted at Saigon's Tan Son Nhut Air Base, with another jump school at Hanoi Bach Mai. The 3e BPVN was formed on 1 September 1952 from Vietnamese cadres of 10e BPC. The 5e BPVN was similarly formed on 1 September 1953 from the Vietnamese cadre of 3e BPC, followed by 7e BPVN on 1 November. Up to this point most officers and senior NCOs were seconded from the French parachute forces. This was to change on 1 March 1954 when the all-Vietnamese 6e BPVN was activated with hand-picked Vietnamese officers and NCOs. Shortly afterwards 3rd Co. Vietnamese Parachute Engrs. was formed.

The Vietnamese parachute battalions were part of the general reserve, as were all French Expeditionary Corps parachute units, though sometimes formed into temporary brigade-sized task forces of Vietnamese and French battalions. The CIPs and BPVNs were to participate in dozens of combat jumps, large and small, with their parent battalions until the French withdrawal. On 20 November 1953 5e BPVN parachuted in with over 4,000 other paras to secure

23

Dien Bien Phu during the largest airborne operation since World War II. Subsequently flown out, it jumped back in on 13 March 1954 as part of the large but piecemeal reinforcement effort; the battalion was totally destroyed when the base fell in May, but was re-established in August 1954.

After the Republic of Vietnam was granted independence in July 1954, the Army of the Republic of Vietnam (ARVN) began to form. As larger formations were assembled from a heterogeneous collection of French-trained and equipped battalions and smaller units, the ARVN Airborne Group (*Lien-Doan Nhay-Du*) was activated on 1 May 1955 at Tan Son Nhut Air Base; located on the north-west outskirts of Saigon, it was to remain the ARVN Airborne's base for the war's duration. The ARVN Airborne Training Center, modelled after the Ft. Benning jump school, was established the same year using the assets of the former French school and co-located with the unit. The Group was composed of

An ARVN paratrooper fires an M79 grenade launcher. He is wearing a locally made vest for the 40mm rounds. (Nguyên Ngoc Hanh)

four of the former BPVNs; they retained their original numbers, but were redesignated Airborne Battalions (*Tiêu-Doan Nhuy-Du*—TDND); 7ᵉ BPVN had been disbanded on 1 March 1955. The 4,000-man Abn. Gp. was composed of the Group HHC, 1st, 3rd, 5th and 6th TDNDs and the Abn. Combat Support Bn. (Engineer and Base Technical cos.; Communications and Air Delivery Support Sections). Each battalion was composed of a headquarters, combat support, and three (later four) rifle companies[1], eventually totalling 1,000 troopers. They were intended as an internal reaction force in the event of a North Korean-style invasion from North Vietnam, then thought to be the most likely threat by American advisors. In addition to combating a growing Communist insurgency, the airborne battalions participated in the suppression of the Binh Xuyen, Cao Dai, and Hoa Hao militant political sects in the Saigon area from late 1954 through early 1956.

[1] Companies were designated by two-digit number (three in 11th TDND's case), the first being the battalion number followed by the company's, e.g. 6th TDND: 60th (HHC), 61st, 62nd, 63rd, 64th (all rifle), and 65th (Combat Support). ARVN Airborne, Ranger, and Marine battalions had four rifle companies, as opposed to three in standard infantry battalions.

On 1 December 1959 the Group was expanded during a general ARVN reorganisation into the Airborne Brigade (*Lu-Doan Nhay-Du*) by the addition of the new 8th and reactivation of the 7th TDNDs. However the Vietnamese Air Force possessed only the 1st and 2nd Transport Sdns. equipped with C-47s (replaced by C-119s in 1968) to lift the Brigade. The ARVN became stronger; and at one point South Vietnam's President Diem even planned to invade the North, using the Brigade to secure a position near North Vietnam's coast to delay advancing enemy forces and allow the evacuation of 'two to three million' Northerners. The Brigade amused itself with activities closer to home, however. In November 1960 three of its battalions surrounded the presidential palace, calling for political reforms and more effective efforts toward eliminating the VC. The coup, led by the brigade commander, failed when loyal ARVN troops arrived and the paratroopers 'surrendered', the coup's leaders fleeing the country. For the remainder of Diem's regime the paratroopers were regarded with distrust.

The Abn. Bde. and later Division were composed entirely of volunteers. They undertook nine weeks of intensive combat training at the Airborne Training Center, followed by a three-week jump school requiring five jumps. Like the Vietnamese Special Forces and Marines, the paratroopers received better pay, rations, quarters, and family benefits than the common ARVN soldier.

The Brigade normally conducted operations with two or three battalions under the control of its two small Task Force HQs (1st and 2nd TFs, to become brigade HHCs in 1969).

An ARVN Abn. Bde. lieutenant armed with an M1A1 carbine waves his men forward. His jumpwings can be seen over his right pocket. (Nguyên Ngoc Hanh)

One battalion was always kept at Tan Son Nhut on airborne alert, capable of parachute or air-landed delivery anywhere in the country within a matter of hours. Battalions rotated this task for the duration of the Brigade's and the later Division's existence. Battalions were also usually rotated to secure Vung Tau, a duty which doubled as an R&R opportunity, leading to it being termed the 'Beach Battalion'. Another battalion was often rotated to Da Nang as a northern reaction force. The Brigade/Division acted as part of the ARVN high command's general reserve, often being committed to many of the most critical actions in the war. They became known throughout the country as 'Angels in Red Hats'.

It was not until 5 March 1962 that the ARVN airborne were to make another combat jump[1]. A battalion was jumped in to reinforce the endangered garrison at Bo Tuc on the Cambodian border. On 14 July two alert battalion companies were dropped in to reinforce an ambushed convoy. Another battalion drop occurred on 2 January 1963 to reinforce the 7th ARVN Inf. Div. at Ap Duc in the Mekong Delta. The battalions also executed heliborne 'Eagle Flight' operations, acting as immediate reaction forces to enemy contacts. In 1965, during the turmoil following Diem's

[1] A complete record of the ARVN Airborne's combat jumps does not exist, and what information is available is often incomplete.

assassination, Brigade units were involved to varying degrees in several coup attempts, usually siding with the current 'government'.

In late July 1965 the 2nd Abn. TF (3rd and 8th TDNDs) were dispatched to the Duc Co Special Forces camp at the termination of Highway 19 on the Cambodian border. Both battalions became heavily engaged with VC Main Force units fighting from a maze of concealed tunnel-connected bunkers. Forced to withdraw, the TF established defensive positions during the night and were attacked before first light. For seven days the TF and camp were subjected to almost continuous mortar, recoilless rifle, and machine-gun fire. Plans were made to parachute the 1st TF in to block the VC between the two forces, but this never materialised. On 3 August the 5th TDND was finally air-landed on the Duc Co strip to reinforce the 2nd TF. A joint ARVN Ranger and Marine force supported by armour fought its way from Pleiku to link up with the TF; almost 500 VC were killed in the course of the operation. In early September 1965 the 1st TF (3rd and 8th TDNDs) parachuted in near Ben Cat while

An ARVN paratrooper carries a wounded VC prisoner, 1968. His jump indicator badge can be made out on his left pocket. (Nguyên Ngoc Hanh)

the 2nd TF (5th and 6th TDNDs) and 173rd US Abn. Bde. attacked from the south. In early October all battalions were air landed at Bong Son and conducted a search-and-destroy operation followed by others with Brigade elements deployed to various areas.

The North Vietnamese escalation of the war led to a further expansion of the ARVN Airborne in 1965. The 2nd TDND was activated on 1 September followed by the 9th on 1 October, both receiving tactical training at the Australian-operated Van Kiep Training Centre. The small 1st Abn. Arty. Bn. was also formed during this period. It was soon proposed to expand the Brigade to a division. Gen. Westmoreland had some reservations due to the unit's sometimes shabby treatment of civilians; he withheld his approval until the Brigade improved its record, which it soon did. The Airborne Division (*Su-Doan Nhay-Du*) was activated on 1 December 1965 and a 3rd TF HQ was added. By 1967 the 11th TDND, 2nd and 3rd Arty. Bns., Recon. Co., three TF/brigade HQs[1], and additional service units had been added giving the Division a strength of 13,000 paratroopers:

Division HHC
1st Abn. TF/Bde. HHC
  1st Abn. Bn.
  8th Abn. Bn.
  9th Abn. Bn.
  1st Abn. Arty. Bn.
2nd Abn. TF/Bde. HHC

A group of ARVN Abn. Div. advisors outfitted in a wide variety of US and ARVN uniforms. The captain at far right in the red beret wears ARVN rank insignia on his shirt opening. Most wear the ARVN jump indicator pocket badge. (Red Hats Assoc.)

  5th Abn. Bn.
  7th Abn. Bn.
  11th Abn. Bn.
  2nd Abn. Arty. Bn.
3rd Abn. TF/Bde. HHC
  2nd Abn. Bn.
  3rd Abn. Bn.
  6th Abn. Bn.
  3rd Abn. Arty. Bn.
Division Troops
  Abn. Signal Bn.
  Abn. Support Bn.[2]
  Abn. Medical Bn.
  Abn. Recon. Co. (later a Bn.)
  Abn. Engr. Co.

The story of the ARVN Airborne would not be complete without mentioning the Division's 162nd Airborne Advisory Detachment, originally the Airborne Brigade Advisory Detachment. Like all major ARVN units the Airborne were assigned a US advisory element. US officers were paired with their Vietnamese counterparts, from the Brigade/Division commander down to company commanders, as well as with

[1] The brigades retained the 'task force' designation until 1969. The assignment of airborne battalions to brigades as listed in the table was standard, but, as with their US counterparts, was often changed as the tactical situation demanded.

[2] HQ and Service, Technical Service, Maintenance, Transportation, Supply, and Finance Companies.

ARVN Abn. Div. advisors in 1966 wearing four different uniforms: (L to R) OG 107 fatigues with sleeves cut short; late pattern ARVN airborne camouflage cut as US fatigues; early pattern ARVN camouflage; and late pattern ARVN airborne camouflage of ARVN cut. (Ralph Garens)

principal staff officers at all levels. US NCOs assisted the staff and company advisors. It was one of the most sought-after of advisory assignments, and only the best advisors went to the Airborne. Extremely good relationships were maintained between the advisors, their counterparts, and units—a situation regrettably not always found in other ARVN units. Just under 1,000 US advisors served with the Brigade and Division receiving on average two awards for valour per tour[1].

In January 1966 a combined operation was conducted with the 173rd Abn. Bde. in the Plain of Reeds. At the end of the month the entire Division was airlifted back to Bong Son, and spent many hard days fighting alongside the 1st Cav. Division. On 3 March 1966 one battalion conducted a parachute raid near Son Cau. A two-battalion task force jumped in Chuong Thien Province for another raid on 27 December

1966, and executed a similar operation there the following year. Operation 'Fairfax', December 1966 to December 1967, was a year-long mission providing security in Gia Dinh Province while ARVN units undertook major retraining to upgrade their capabilities. The 3rd and 5th TDNDs participated along with the 5th ARVN Ranger Gp. and units of the 1st, 4th and 25th US Inf. Divisions. The Division's battalions were constantly sent at short notice to aid remote outposts and endangered units throughout Vietnam and to exploit enemy contacts initiated by other units.

The Tet-68 offensive found the 9th TDND defending Quang Tri City. The 3rd, 7th and 9th TDNDs were later committed to retaking Hue's Citadel in a vicious fight. The 3rd, 6th and 8th TDNDs participated in the April 1968 relief of the US Marines at Khe Sanh. Division units also took part in Operation 'Delaware' in the A Shau Valley with the 1st Cav. and 101st Abn. Divs. in May and April. The 7th TDND, on airborne alert, was pitched into the second battle of Saigon in May. On 17 November 1968 a battalion was jumped into IV CTZ's Seven Mountains region to aid the 5th Mobile Strike Force with its clearing operations. In 1969 Division units were again called on to aid the defence of Saigon and Tay Ninh City in III CTZ. Other battalions fought throughout Vietnam.

The allied incursion into Cambodia from 29 April to 30 June 1970 found Division units committed to this effort to

---

[1] As a personal note the author would like to say that all the former US advisors and ARVN paratroopers interviewed emphasised that good co-operation and harmonious relationships were the norm. The advisors without exception stated that the posting was one of the high points of their careers.

destroy the enemy's favoured sanctuary and massive supply bases. 'Lam Son 719' was a principally ARVN operation designed to destroy NVA bases in Laos from 30 January to 6 April 1971, and the best ARVN formations were committed to this principally Vietnamese show. The Airborne and 1st ARVN Inf. Divs. helicopter inserted battalions into Laos, establishing fire support bases, with the 1st ARVN Armour Brigade forcing a ground link-up. ARVN Rangers and Marines provided a back-up, and massive helicopter support came from the 101st Abn. Division. The Airborne commander felt that tying his paratroopers down in static fire support bases was a serious misuse of an aggressive manoeuvre force. His assessment was correct; the 3rd Bde. HQ and 3rd TDND were overrun, and only the timely arrival of the 8th TDND and an armour squadron prevented the annihilation of the 2nd TDND. 'Lam Son 719' was a mixed success; the NVA supply bases were destroyed and their planned offensive into South Vietnam was delayed for a year, but ARVN losses were high.

The NVA's 1972 Easter Offensive into Quang Tri Province again saw the Airborne thrown into the fray. The Division's final jump was executed on 4 May when an element descended on Chu Pao Pass to open the Pleiku–Kontum Road. The Abn. Div. was airlifted to the neighbouring Thua Thien Province in late June; it counter-attacked, driving the NVA back to Quang Tri City, which it helped to retake in late July. The Division had suffered extensive losses, and was placed in defensive positions to receive replacements and new equipment. The Division's morale suffered greatly from being kept in a defensive posture, and from the fact that their families in the south were in financial straits due to the deteriorating economic situation brought on by the US withdrawal. Some troopers deserted, and morale dwindled further. Finally, in late October, the Division, supported by the 7th Ranger Gp., resumed the attack north.

Early 1973 again found the Division on the defensive when withdrawn to Hue for rest. This was short-lived, as the NVA resumed their attacks through the northern provinces. In August 1973 the 1st Abn. Bde. was sent to Da Nang to bolster the defences of the 3rd ARVN Inf. Div. The 3rd Abn. Bde. was later sent to Da Nang as well. The 2nd Abn. Bde. remained in Thua Thien Province attached to the ARVN Marine Div. The ARVN Airborne now had its own version of the 101st's 'Hamburger Hill' experience. Hill 1062 north of Thuong Duc in Quang Nam Province was occupied by the NVA. The 1st Abn. Bde. (8th and 9th TDNDs) began the attack on 18 August. A see-saw battle developed, with the hill changing hands on several occasions until it was finally secured in December. Seven of the Division's battalions were eventually committed, with a loss of 500 dead and 2,000 wounded. The NVA suffered 2,000 dead and 5,000 wounded. Since its deployment to the northern provinces in May 1972 the Division had lost almost 2,900 dead, 12,000 wounded, 300 missing, and many of its best leaders. Replacements were inexperienced; but the Division continued in being.

Early 1974 again saw the Division in the defence of northern Quang Tri Province with the NVA relentlessly applying pressure. The brigades were shifted around to meet new NVA threats throughout the year, fighting many hilltop battles. The 3rd Abn. Bde. was sent to Quang Nam Province in January 1975. The ARVN were able to drive the NVA from most populated areas in the northern provinces by March. The enemy then opened what was to become the

Colonel Bao (later killed in action), an ARVN Abn. Div. staff officer, with NVA POWs in the background. He is armed with a .38-calibre revolver in a shoulder holster, typical armament for staff officers. (Red Hats Assoc.)

final offensive on the heels of this success. On 12 March the Division was ordered to begin moving to Saigon by sea. The 2nd and 3rd Abn. Bdes. were diverted to II Corps, however; and the exhausted and greatly understrength units fought their final battles against overwhelming NVA forces in Phuoc Tuy Province in the Central Highlands. The 1st Abn. Bde. was expended, with the 18th ARVN Inf. Div. and Ranger battalions, at Xuan Loc in III Corps. The once-proud ARVN Airborne battalions were mere shells of their former selves, but, with other scattered ARVN units, they fought to the very end.

In addition to the many Vietnamese unit awards, eight of the nine TDNDs (8th TDND twice) and the three brigade HQs were awarded the US Presidential Unit Citation. With its many Vietnamese and French awards, the ARVN Airborne was the most highly decorated of ARVN formations.

For years after the downfall of the Saigon government, Vietnamese refugees spoke of surviving groups of ARVN paratroopers fighting an unsupported guerrilla war in the hills and jungles of the former III Corps area.

ARVN Special Forces

The predecessor of Vietnamese Airborne Special Forces was formed on 1 November 1957 when 44 men trained by the US 14th Special Forces Operational Det. were selected as the cadre for the 300-man 1st Observation Gp. (also known as Joint Reconnaissance Unit I). This was a Special Forces-type unit concentrating on the LRRP and guerrilla rôles, and tasked with organising behind-the-lines guerrilla units in the event of an invasion from the North. These personnel were from among 70 originally chosen in early 1957 to undertake airborne and radio operator training prior to receiving commando training from the US Special Forces (USSF). Headquartered at Nha Trang, the Group was subordinate to the Presidential Liaison (later Survey) Office, under President Diem's direct command. Support came from the US Military Assistance Program (MAP) with training provided by the CIA. The following year it was moved to Saigon during Diem's attempt to consolidate his power, and its strength grew to 400. Initially it was nothing more than a 'palace guard', contributing little to the war effort. Some reconnaissance missions were conducted on the Laotian border in 1960. Elements were deployed to Quang Tri Province with the 1st ARVN Inf. Div. to halt infiltration from North Vietnam in 1961. In October 1961 the Group began executing reconnaissance and interdiction operations against the NVA in the Laotian panhandle. On 1 November 1961 it was redesignated the 77th Group in imitation of the earlier US 77th SFGA and its mission expanded. Its advisory assistance now came from the USSF, and a few agents were sent into North Vietnam. In addition to its covert operations it was to become more involved with counterinsurgency operations. Operation 'Lei-Yu' ('Eagle'), a counterinsurgency effort, was initiated with a night parachute infiltration into the swamps of Binh Hung in early 1962, and lasted until mid-1962.

A variety of counterinsurgency and paramilitary programmes were established in 1962 under the US Military Assistance Advisory Command Vietnam and the CIA's US Operations Mission. This unco-ordinated collection of organisations was consolidated into the Civilian Irregular Defense Group (CIDG, pronounced 'cidge') programme on 1 July 1963. The USSF, originally tasked with running most of these programmes for the administering agencies, was given the mission of supporting and advising the CIDG. In early 1963 Diem ordered the Presidential Survey Office to restructure the 77th Group, bringing it more into line with USSF projects. The 77th was reorganised and the new 31st Group was formed on 1 February 1963 in Saigon, to undergo a year's training from the USSF. To control both groups the Airborne Special Forces Command (*Nhay-Du Luc-Luong Dac-Biêt*) was formed on 15 March in Saigon; it was more commonly known simply as the Special Forces (*Luc-Luong Dac-Biêt*—LLDB). It was soon relocated to Nha Trang, along with Headquarters USSF Vietnam (Provisional), in order to be in a more central location.

The LLDB were placed in command of the CIDG, with the USSF acting as their advisors as well as controlling all funds, supplies, and equipment. This USSF control of critical resources explains why the CIDG programme was so success-

ARVN Abn. Div. jump-qualified nurses await a presentation ceremony for Gen. Westmoreland's wife. They wear the Division's patch on the right shoulder, since they were only attached. The Division prided itself on its hospital and the medical care provided for its troops. (Red Hats Assoc.)

ful. LLDB officers were still rated as Presidential Survey Officers. President Diem was assassinated on 1 November 1963, and the LLDB quickly fell out of the favour it had long enjoyed. On 5 January 1964 the LLDB Command was removed from the control of the now defunct Presidential Survey Office and made an independent command, almost a separate branch of service, under the Joint General Staff. The 31st LLDB Gp., its training completed, was moved to Dong Ba Thin on 25 February 1964 and given control of all LLDB teams in I and II CTZs. The 77th LLDB Gp. remained in Saigon's Camp Hung Vuong from where it commanded teams in III and IV CTZs. On 1 September 1964 the 31st 77th Groups were redesignated the 111th and 301st LLDB Groups respectively. The LLDB now had over 2,600 personnel assigned.

In April 1964 the Vietnamese formed the Special Exploitation Service, responsible for covert intelligence and special mission activities, and the Vietnamese contribution to the Military Assistance Command Vietnam's Studies and Observation Group (MACV-SOG). This separated the LLDB from special missions, allowing them to concentrate solely on the CIDG programme. USSF Vietnam (Provisional) was inactivated and the 5th SFGA assumed its missions on 1 October 1964. Both LLDB groups were dissolved in late 1965, and the LLDB Command was reorganised along lines similar to a USSF group to make its structure more compatible to its USSF counterpart group. The LLDB Command (Augmented), authorised 3,322 personnel in 1968, was now composed of the Command HQ, HQ and Service Co.; 66oth Signal Co.; LLDB Training Center (at Dong Ba Thin); 81st Abn. Ranger Bn.; and four C-, 12 B- and over 70 A-teams.

One C-team (*Toán*) was assigned in each of the corps tactical zones to control a varied number of A- and B-teams co-located with USSF counterpart teams. An LLDB A-team was responsible for the command of each CIDG Camp Strike Force, a battalion-sized light irregular counterinsurgency unit. Other LLDB elements were assigned to the Mobile Strike Forces and various special reconnaissance projects. By 1968 the LLDB had control over almost 40,000 CIDG in the Camp and Mobile Strike Forces, and reconnaissance projects. Over 4,000 Regional Forces and 5,500 Popular Forces troops were also under the LLDB in I CTZ[1]. Little known even to many USSF personnel, the LLDB did operate some Camp Strike Forces without a counterpart USSF team.

The USSF acted as advisors to the LLDB administering the CIDG programme[2]. Admittedly the 'marriage' was not always harmonious, though good working relationships were more common than not. Cultural differences, individual training and proficiency differentials, basic motivations, and the differences in the two organisations' outlook on the war did lead to many disagreements and misunderstandings. It was not unusual for the LLDB to run day-to-day camp administration and the USSF to control the combat operations, though usually permitting the LLDB at least to have the appearance of exercising command over the CIDG. LLDB personnel were also involved in the various non-MACV-SOG special reconnaissance projects including 'Delta' (Det. B-52), 'Sigma' (Det. B-56), and 'Gamma' (Det. B-57).

An LLDB A-team commander and his USSF counterpart review an operation plan, 1968. (Green Beret Magazine)

The LLDB were volunteers with prior service in combat units, many with the Airborne or Rangers. However, most officers had used some degree of 'political' connection to win the assignment. There were a very small number of Montagnard LLDB officers, but for the most part the Vietnamese were highly prejudiced against minority groups and restricted non-Vietnamese from entry. Their training, though not as in-depth as the USSF's, was undertaken at the Dong Ba Thin LLDB Training Center advised by USSF Det. B-1, later B-51. All were airborne qualified and given some degree of English language instruction, though this was not always apparent to the USSF. Modelled on the USSF's own training, the course began with four weeks of basic SF skills followed by training in one of six SF job skills: operations and intelligence, demolitions, light weapons, heavy weapons, communications, or medical. A two-week 'live-fire' field exercise completed the course. Fourteen additional advanced courses ranging from anti-tank warfare to Tai Kwon Do were also offered.

They enjoyed higher pay and better ration benefits, and their families were allowed to accompany them to their assignments—an important benefit from the Vietnamese viewpoint, though one not always taken up due to the exposed location of the camps. It was not popular among Vietnamese to serve in remote, primitive outposts with Montagnards and other 'savages' and this led to further difficulties in recruiting qualified LLDB volunteers.

One unit subordinate to the LLDB Command deserves special note. The 81st Abn. Ranger Bn. (*Tiêu-Doan Biêt-Cach Nhay-Du*) was Project 'Delta's' reaction and exploitation force. Project 'Delta' was a special reconnaissance organisation tasked with intelligence collection, artillery and air strike target acquisition, bomb damage assessment, direct action missions, and hunter/killer operations. The 81st was assigned directly to the LLDB Command and not to the Ranger Command like all other ARVN Ranger units, which were non-airborne. Most of the Battalion's personnel were trained at the Duc My Ranger Training Center and received their parachute and tactical training at the LLDB Training Center. The Battalion's officers were LLDB advised by USSF

---

[1] Collectively known as the RF/PF ('Ruff-Puffs'), the RFs were local defence forces under provincial control and the PFs were employed in their village or hamlet.

[2] See Elite 4, *US Army Special Forces 1952–84* for additional information on the USSF's involvement with the LLDB and the CIDG programme.

LLDB and USSF personnel make final plans prior to an operation: Bu Prang Camp, 1967. (Green Beret Magazine)

officers and NCOs of Project 'Delta's' Battalion Advisory Section.

Originally formed as the 91st Abn. Ranger Bn. on 1 November 1964, it had three companies with a fourth added in 1965. In late 1966 it was purged of non-Vietnamese in an effort to make it more effective and redesignated the 81st. It was then expanded to a 31-man headquarters and six 134-man companies. Normally four companies were dedicated to Project 'Delta' support and the others retained under LLDB control.

Not widely known until 1968, the Battalion was called to retake Saigon's Gia Dinh section in June. Although unaccustomed to urban combat, the 81st handled itself well and aggressively cleared the NVA from their fortified rubble positions. The Battalion's principal mission was to provide airmobile reaction forces to aid in the extraction of recon. teams and execute immediate exploitation raids on targets discovered by the teams. It was also used to reinforce SF camps under siege. In late 1972 the Battalion was attached to the Special Mission Service.

The CIDG programme was terminated on 31 December 1970. Many of the Strike Forces, 14,000 troops, were transferred to the ARVN and converted to a new organisation, the Border Rangers, with others being made RF/PF units. The LLDB was dissolved on 1 January 1971 with many of its personnel assuming command of the 37 Border Ranger Battalions and the others transferred to ARVN combat units,

especially the Airborne Div. and Ranger Command. The best of the LLDB were integrated into the Special Mission Service under the Vietnamese Strategic Technical Directorate, the successor of the Special Exploitation Service. Their retraining for reconnaissance missions began on 1 February 1971 and lasted for a full year before they became operational. This organisation was disbanded in November 1972.

Mobile Strike Forces

The US 5th Special Forces Group (Airborne) formed its first Mobile Strike Forces in July 1965. The concept was derived from the 'Eagle Flight', a platoon-sized heliborne reaction force raised the previous October in Pleiku and led by Det. A-334B (a split A-team). They were more commonly referred to as simply MIKE Forces, the acronym for Mobile strIKE. The MIKE Forces were formed to provide US Special Forces camps within each of Vietnam's four CTZs with a 598-man, three-company reaction force and limited special operations-capable battalion, though it was well into 1967 before all reached full strength. Each was advised and led by a USSF A-team (SF Operational Detachment A); it was not until the following year that an LLDB A-team was assigned, upon the insistence of the LLDB. The MIKE Forces were directly subordinate to the C-team responsible for USSF elements in each CTZ. A fifth MIKE Force, formed in February 1966 at the same time as the IV Corps unit, was directly under control of the 5th SFGA and tasked with countrywide employment. Its rôle was to back up the corps MIKE Forces as well as to execute independent operations throughout the country.

1: PFC, 1st Bde., 101st Abn. Div., 1965
2: Sgt., 3d Bde., 82d Abn. Div., 1968
3: S/Sgt., 173d Abn. Bde., 1971

A

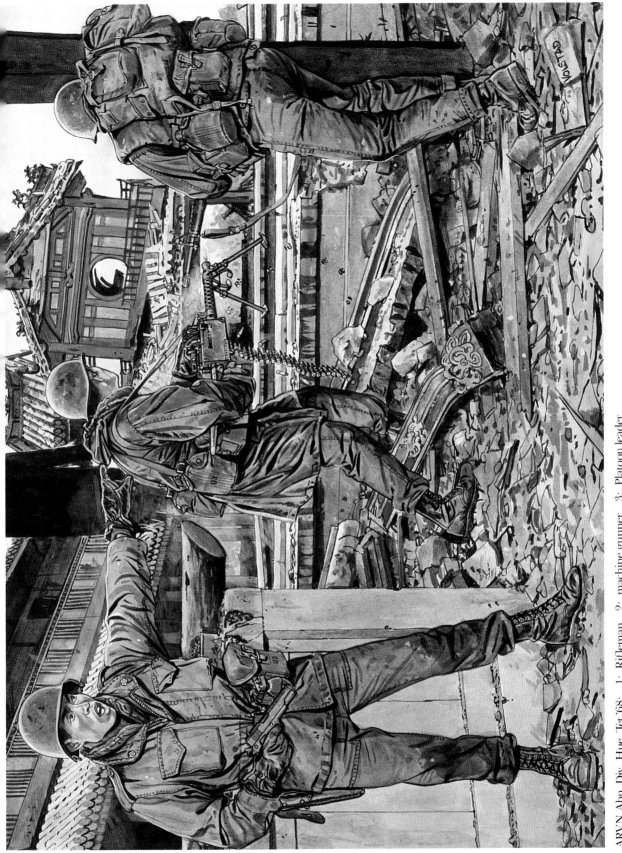

ARVN Abn. Div., Hue, Tet '68:   1: Rifleman   2: machine gunner   3: Platoon leader

C

1: Marine scout, 1st Force Recon. Co., 1965
2: Patrol leader, 3d Force Recon. Co., 1971
3: Pathfinder, 25th Aviation Bn., 1969
4: Pathfinder, 1st Aviation Bn., 1970

D

1: Capt., ARVN LLDB, 1970
2: Sgt., 91st Abn. Ranger Bn., 1967
3: Striker, 5th MIKE Force, 1967

E

1: Rifleman, ARVN Abn. Gp., 1955
2: Sgt., ARVN Abn. Bde., 1963
3: 1st Lt., ARVN Abn. Div., 1972
4: Paratrooper, ARVN Abn. Div.

F

1: Patrol Commander, Australian SAS
2: Patrol 2ic, ASAS
3: Signaller, ASAS
4: Medic, ASAS
5: Troop Commander, NZSAS

G

VOLSTAD

1: Sgt., 1st LRRP Tp., Royal Thai
'Black Panther' Div.
2,3: Cpl., 350th NVA Abn. Bde.

H

Jumpwings: see text commentaries for identifications

1

2

3

4

5

6

7

8

9

10

11

12

13

14

15

I

1

2

3

4

5

6

ARVN Airborne shoulder patches: see text commentaries for identifications

J

US Army Airborne patches and crests: see text commentaries for identifications

1: T-10 Main Parachute
2: T-10R Reserve Parachute
3: M1950 Adjustable Individual
Weapons Case
4: Weapons & Individual
Equipment Container
5: Kit bag & H-harness

L

CTZ	A-Team	Location
I	A-113	Da Nang
II	A-219	Pleiku
III	A-302	Bien Hoa
IV	A-430	Don Phuc
All	A-503	Nha Trang

It had been found early in the war that US Army, Marine, and ARVN formations were sometimes—tragically—unable or unwilling to aid endangered USSF camps. MIKE Force elements could be rapidly airlifted to a camp's vicinity and parachuted in or landed by helicopter. Once on the ground they could internally reinforce the defending Camp Strike Force, externally counterattack an enemy siege force, or occupy key dominating terrain in the vicinity to prevent its use by the enemy. They also conducted independent tactical operations of their own; or the entire unit, certain battalions, or companies could come under the operational control of regular US Army divisions or brigades. Elements were also occasionally attached to USSF special project B-teams or Camp Strike Force B- and A-teams.

In early 1968 the Nha Trang MIKE Force was increased to six companies, and later nine, without a battalion organisation. Additionally, in II CTZ, the Camp Strike Force B-teams (B-22, 23, 24) maintained their own usually company-sized MIKE Forces for local use until April 1969. Gradually all MIKE Forces were enlarged to between two and five 552-man battalions, a 227-man headquarters and service company (HSC), and a 135-man recon. company. The Nha Trang (5th) MIKE Force had no recon. company, but rather two recon. platoons as part of its 336-man HSC. The 4th MSF was authorised a 184-man airboat company in November 1968. There were also such units as security and training companies, which varied over the years. MIKE Force strength ranged from 1,400 to 3,000 Strikers. Additional personnel were assigned to the MIKE Forces' A-teams to control the enlarged units.

A special operations organisation, not to be confused with the MIKE Forces, was the non-airborne Mobile Guerrilla Forces (MGF). These were generally small task forces comprising a separate strike company augmented with a recon. platoon and led by a reduced strength A-team with USSF NCOs as platoon leaders, and totalling from 150 to 200 Strikers. Their mission was to take the war into secluded VC strongholds, areas where Free World forces seldom ventured and which were often out of artillery range. These were long-term missions requiring the MGF to be resupplied by air. Operating in a manner similar to the VC, the MGFs would covertly infiltrate an enemy sanctuary and execute ambushes and raids, as well as directing air strikes on unsuspecting base camps and supply routes. With the expansion of the MIKE Forces, the MGF's strength was absorbed into them. The MIKE Forces were now additionally tasked with MGF-type missions, though usually larger, in the form of 'Blackjack' operations.

LLDB and USSF instructors teach firing techniques at the LLDB Training Center, 1968. LLDB students wore tiger-stripe uniforms rather than the LLDB-pattern camouflage. (Green Beret Magazine)

An LLDB first lieutenant demonstrates the proper exit position to an LLDB student at Dong Ba Thin LLDB Training Center, 1968. (Green Beret Magazine)

On 23 May 1968 a B-team was assigned to each MIKE Force, and additional A-teams were authorised to control each battalion and the increased number of companies. Det. B-36, III Corps MIKE Force, was formed from the B-36 Special Forces Task Force, originally tasked with special reconnaissance missions. Collectively the USSF B- and A-teams and the lone LLDB A-team were referred to as the Mobile Strike Force Command (MSFC), while the entire force was simply the Mobile Strike Force (MSF). Initially these were designated after the B-team's number, e.g. 36th MSFC, but on 29 June 1968 the second digit was dropped from the designation. Generally they were more popularly known as, for example, II Corps MIKE Force.

In most cases the LLDB were mere figureheads, though nominally they commanded the MIKE Force and the USSF were to be advisors only. In actuality the USSF B-team commander, a lieutenant-colonel in Vietnam after 1968, was the MSFC commander, while his 20 or so officers and NCOs doubled as the regimental staff, supervised the various headquarters and service company's platoons, and led the recon. company. The A-team commanders, captains, commanded the battalions; lieutenants and NCOs ran the rifle companies.

The enlarged MIKE Forces were fully developed by 1969:

MSF	CTZ	Units	Location
1st	I	HSC, 2 Bns., Recon. Co.	Da Nang
2nd	II	HSC, 5 Bns., Recon. Co.	Pleiku*
3rd	III	HSC, 3 Bns., Recon.Co.	Long Hai
4th	IV	HSC, 3 Bns., Recon.Co., Airboat Co.	Can Tho
5th	All	HSC, 4 Bns., 105mm Plt.	Nha Trang

In 1969 the MSFCs were comprised of the following USSF elements:

MSFC	B-team	A-teams
1st	B-16	A-111, 113
2nd	B-20	A-204*, 217, 218, 219, 223
3rd	B-36	A-302, 303, 304
4th	B-40	A-401, 402, 403, 404†
5th	B-55	A-551, 552, 553, 554

*4th MSF Bn., Kontum.
†Airboat Company.

The troops making up the MIKE Forces were specially trained CIDG personnel. They were recruited, trained, uniformed, equipped, fed, and paid by the USSF. The Strikers were not part of the ARVN, but for all practical purposes were 'civilian' employees of the US government. Various ethnic groups were recruited into the MIKE Forces, their ethnic composition changing from time to time in some units. Generally speaking, however, the 1st, 2nd, and 5th were primarily Montagnard, though some Chinese Nungs and Vietnamese served in the latter two; Cambodians and Nungs made up the 3rd and 4th, again with some Vietnamese in the 3rd.

Due to their mission the MIKE Forces were trained in a more conventional rôle than their Camp Strike Force counterparts. This meant training for larger scale and more complex missions of longer duration; they were also more heavily armed. Many of the Strikers were recruited from Camp Strike Forces and others fresh off the streets or rice paddies. Most training was conducted within the units, but some were trained at CIDG Training Centers located in each CTZ. An example of early unit training is seen in the II Corps MIKE Force's programme at Pleiku: seven weeks basic, six weeks advanced infantry, and one week airborne training with two qualifying jumps.

USSF Det. B-51 ran the LLDB Training Center at Dong Ba Thin, established in April 1964. Here a jump school was operated capable of turning out at least a parachute-qualified company per month, along with a MIKE Force Training Center. This was moved to Hon Tre Island near Na Trang in September 1968, but returned to Dong Ba Thin in October 1969. Most of the parachute instruction was accomplished by LLDB, but augmented with USSF NCOs, many of whom had been jump instructors at Ft. Benning. Some of the MIKE Forces conducted their own local jump schools as well. Non airborne-qualified US administrative and support personnel assigned to the 5th SEGA were given the opportunity to attend this course, which maintained somewhat harsher training and disciplinary standards than Ft. Benning. By no means all MIKE Force personnel were airborne qualified, though some units did at times reach near 100 per cent qualification. This usually lasted until the first major operation, when casualties quickly reduced those so qualified. Personnel turnover was a continuing problem as well; it was not unusual in the later years for a given MIKE Force to field only two or three airborne-qualified companies.

MIKE Force combat operations tended to be brutal. Their independent operations were often executed in some of the most hotly contested areas, while the camp relief missions turned into gruelling slugging matches against determined and well dug-in enemy forces. In both instances the MIKE Forces were pitted against hardened NVA and VC main force units.

MIKE Force companies and battalions constantly conducted operations throughout their corps' areas in their efforts to seek out and destroy the elusive enemy. Camp relief operations were common, as were independent sweeps and combined operations with US, ARVN, and other Free World Forces. They were also employed to secure camps under construction until a local strike force was recruited and trained. A large number of major independent operations were also mounted. The many camp battles in II CTZ were the focus of the II Corps MIKE Force, these often turning into prolonged fights to secure critical hilltops, repulse enemy assaults, and finally to drive the NVA/VC from the vicinity. The Nha Trang MIKE Force became adept at fighting in IV CTZ's rocky VC strongholds in the Seven Mountains, Nui Coto, and elsewhere. The III Corps MIKE Force often became bitterly engaged with its arch enemy, the 5th VC Div. in War Zones C and D. They were also committed to the Cambodia operation in May 1970. The I and IV Corps MIKE Forces conducted countless operations to secure exposed border camps.

The MIKE Forces conducted more combat jumps than any other organisation in Vietnam, with the exception of the ARVN Airborne. The first was on 2 April 1967, when 39 USSF and 314 Strikers of the Nha Trang MIKE Force jumped in to secure the Bunard SF camp under construction in III CTZ. On 13 May they again jumped in with 20 USSF and 374 Strikers during the operation to take IV CTZ's Nui Gai Mountain. The II Corps MIKE Force executed its only combat jump when 11 USSF and 37 Strikers of a pathfinder element led the way for 50 USSF and 275 Strikers in the main force to secure a new camp site at Bu Prang on 5 October. The final MIKE Force combat jump occurred on 17 November 1968 when the Nha Trang Force inserted approximately 25 USSF and 495 Strikers in the Seven Mountains area during one of the many IV CTZ hill battles.

After years of valiant service the MIKE Forces were closed down in 1970–71. I Corps' was converted into Border Rangers in November 1970; II Corps' met the same end in May. IV Corps' was disbanded in May 1970, the Nha Trang Force in December 1970, and III Corps' in January 1971, after being reduced to battalion size the year before. Some of its assets were used to form the US Army Individual Training Gp.s (UITG), later *Forces Armée Nationale Khmer* Training Command (FANK), to train Cambodian troops.

ANZAC Special Air Service

The Australian and New Zealand SAS, along with other national units, have been extremely active in supporting their nations' commitments to both South-East Asian Treaty

Members of the 81st Airborne Ranger Bn. escort VC suspects, 1968. One Ranger carries evidence in the form of an RPG-2 rocket launcher. (Green Beret Magazine)

Organization (SEATO) and Commonwealth missions in their backyards. To further demonstrate their commitment both nations deployed SAS units to Vietnam in 1966 and 1968 respectively. Specialising in small-scale reconnaissance and ambush patrols, the ASAS and NZSAS troopers proved themselves as some of the most versatile and capable of jungle fighters.

Australian SAS

1 SAS Company, Australian SAS was formed in July 1957 at Swanbourne, Western Australia, with a cadre of personnel drawn from regular units. In 1960 1 SAS Co. was made a component of the Royal Australian Regt. (RAR), until 1 SAS Regt. was formed in September 1964. The new regiment was composed of a Headquarters, Base Sdn., attached elements of 152 Sdn. (Signal), and 1 and 2 SAS Sdns.—the 'sabre' squadrons. SAS sabre squadrons were composed of a headquarters and four 16-man troops.

ASAS training was, and is, modelled on that of the British SAS, with some unique differences. Training included a rigorous initial selection programme emphasizing cross-country land navigation incorporated with lengthy, timed, full-equipment endurance marches. Many months of subsequent specialist training placed emphasis on patrolling, weapons, demolitions, sabotage, communications, medical, small boat, assault swimming, tracking, survival, and jungle combat skills. Most of the training was conducted in Western Australia's tropical forests and deserts; parachute training was conducted at the Royal Australian Air Force Base, Williamtown, New South Wales under the School of Land/Air Warfare. Nine jumps were required to qualify in the three-week basic course, and selected individuals could take the three-and-a-half-week Free Fall Course.

In February 1965 1 Sdn. was deployed to Brunei (the British protectorate in Borneo) to operate against Indonesian forces in conjunction with the British and New Zealand SAS; 2 Sdn. replaced 1 Sdn. at the end of 1965. In November 1966, after conducting many cross-border reconnaissance and ambush missions into neighbouring Sarawak, Australian

Two 81st Airborne Ranger Bn. members, wearing LLDB camouflage and the LLDB patch, prepare a meal in the field, 1968. (Green Beret Magazine)

and New Zealand SAS units were withdrawn. In 1962 six 1 SAS Co. members (one officer, five NCOs) were sent to Vietnam with the Australian Army Training Team, Vietnam (AATTV). Individual ASAS personnel were attached to Special Forces teams to work with the CIDG programme in both Mobile and Camp Strike Forces. In early 1966 3 Sdn. was formed (principally from 1 Sdn. personnel with Borneo experience) specifically for service in Vietnam and deployed there in April. 4 Sdn., with a reinforcement rôle, was soon formed. The other three SAS Squadrons, minus one troop (a fourth NZSAS troop was attached from the end of 1968) subsequently served two approximately one-year tours:

Sdn.	Troops	Tour	Operations
3	I, J, K	16 June 66–25 July 67	134
1	A, B, C	2 Mar. 67–26 Feb. 68	246
2	E, G, H	29 Jan. 68–4 Mar. 69	265
3	I, J, L	3 Feb. 69–18 Feb. 70	?
1	A, B, C	18 Feb. 70–18 Feb. 71	330
2	E, F, G	26 Feb. 71–15 Oct. 71	167

The tours usually overlapped, enabling the relieving squadron to familiarise itself with the area of operations and acclimatise prior to taking over its LRRP mission in support of 1 Australian Task Force (1 ATF)—a brigade-sized combat force which included the battalion-sized New Zealand 'V' Force. Squadrons would 'train-up' prior to deployment, conducting exercises in Australia, Borneo, and Papua New Guinea. Based at Nui Dat Mountain south-east of Saigon, the ASAS were assigned a tactical area of responsibility (TAOR) in III CTZ's Phuoc Tuy Province. Originally 3 Sdn. established its base at the foot of Nui Dat, but after 1 Squadron's arrival it was relocated on to the mountain itself in March 1967.

The ASAS quickly adapted the jungle skills learned in Borneo and Malaysia to the more intense Vietnam environment, although there were some difficulties in the conduct of combined operations with more conventionally minded American units. They were, however, able to work more effectively with the US Navy SEALs in the Mekong Delta, ARVN Rangers, and USSF (principally Project 'Delta' and Det. B-53). They also worked with the US 9th Inf. and 101st Abn. Divisions' LRRP (later Ranger) companies, though their operational techniques were very different. Waterborne patrol insertions were sometimes conducted in conjunction with the US Navy, launching Gemini inflatable boats from destroyers and patrol boats. The ASAS also participated in instructional patrols at the AATTV-operated Van Kiep Training Centre where Vietnamese combat units were trained. Former ASAS members were the principal instructors in the Van Kiep LRRP Training Wing. ASAS personnel were also detached from the resident squadron to serve in the Australian Embassy Guard.

The roughly 100-man ASAS sabre squadrons deployed to Vietnam consisted of a headquarters, signal troop from 152 Sdn., and three troops—one of the squadron's original four troops was disbanded prior to its deployment to Vietnam. Troops, commanded by lieutenants, originally had four four-man patrols (commander, scout, signaller, medic), one doubling as the troop headquarters and led by the troop commander. After 3 Sdn. arrived in-country a fifth man, a

LLDB and USSF II Corps MIKE Force commanders display the banner presented to them on the drop zone during the Bu Prang jump, 5 October 1967. (Green Beret Magazine)

second-in-command, was added to each patrol; and a sixth man was usually attached when executing ambush operations. In April 1967, when reinforcement personnel were allotted from 4 Sdn., a fifth patrol was formed, this one led by the troop sergeant. In early 1970 National Servicemen (conscripts), agreeing to three years service, began to be accepted by the ASAS, a condition forced on the Regiment by the scarcity of professionals as the Australian commitment in Vietnam increased. These troopers, while trained in SAS patrol skills, were not given the full course of advanced specialist training. At the end of 1971 the Training Sdn. was formed within the Regiment, leading to the disbandment of 2 Sdn. after departing Vietnam from its second tour.

Besides its principal mission of patrol-sized LRRP operations, the ASAS also executed troop-sized and larger ambushes, raids, and cordon and searches. The squadrons occasionally conducted annual continuation parachute jumps to maintain their proficiency. On 12 December 1969 3 Sdn., including NZSAS Patrols, conducted a squadron-sized (90 men) jump in the eastern part of their TAOR. Operation 'Stirling' was supported by 35 Sdn., Royal Australian Air Force C-7 Caribou transports. The ASAS considered the operation a 'jolly'; it was actually a deception to cover the infiltration of four to five patrols while the other troops

returned to base. Under the guise of a continuation jump, the drop zone had been secured by B Sdn., 3 Australian Cav. Regt. armoured personnel carriers the day before. The patrols actually being infiltrated linked up with the APCs for transport to their areas of operation.

Throughout their tours the squadrons relied heavily on insertion and extraction support provided by the 16 UH-1B helicopters of 9 Helicopter (Utility) Sdn., Royal Australian Air Force, which included New Zealand crews. Similar support was also provided by the US 135th Aviation Co., which included integrated Australian air and ground crews—the only unit of this kind. The preferred helicopter insertion method was by winch; rapelling was officially adopted during 2 Squadron's first tour, but seldom used. Patrol recovery was often by extraction rope.

The ASAS squadrons and their approximately 600 troopers inflicted over 750 confirmed enemy kills during their five-year Vietnam involvement—especially noteworthy when one considers that their primary task was reconnaissance. Like most reconnaissance units in Vietnam, both the

The 5th and 6th Companies, 5th MIKE Force are presented battle streamers for the battle of Nha Trang during the Tet-68 offensive. The tiger-stripe MIKE Force beret is worn by all Strikers. The MIKE Forces had by now evolved into professional formations with their own traditions and lineages. (Green Beret Magazine)

ASAS and NZSAS experienced the frustration of having reports disbelieved by 1 ATF and other higher allied headquarters. ASAS elements were withdrawn in October 1971, several months before other Australian combat units. ASAS losses were surprisingly small in the light of their mission and length of service: one man died of wounds after evacuation to Australia, one was accidentally killed while disposing of explosives, two succumbed to illness, and two were killed by 'friendlies' when mistaken for enemy. One of the six Australian servicemen still listed missing is a member of 3 Sdn., who fell from a helicopter extraction rope[1]. A total of 52 men were wounded in action. No unit awards were bestowed on the ASAS, but a number of individual decorations were presented: four Military Crosses, two Distinguished Conduct Medals, four Military Medals, and 20 Mentions in Dispatches (two SAS members being twice 'Mentioned', the only Australian soldiers in Vietnam to have that distinction).

New Zealand SAS

The company-sized Independent New Zealand SAS Squadron was raised in June 1955 as that army's first parachute unit. In December it was sent to Malaya and placed

[1] Private D. J. E. Fisher, 27 September 1969.

under the British 22 SAS as simply 'NZ Squadron'. Though effective, the unit was disbanded when it returned home in December 1957, principally for budgetary reasons. In December 1959 the SAS Troop was activated at Papakura Army Camp, and enlarged to 1st NZSAS Sdn. the following year; training assistance was provided by the ASAS. A Territorial (reserve) troop was formed in 1961.

In May 1962 a 30-man NZSAS detachment deployed to Thailand to participate in a combined SEATO exercise and present a show of force in Thailand's troubled north-eastern region during the Laotian crisis. Part of the detachment, 1 Troop, worked with the 1st Battle Gp., 27th Inf., 25th US Inf. Div. at Ban Chanthuk. It later moved to Chiang Mai to work with the USSF. The other element, 3 Troop, trained with the US Special Forces at Udorn. Both troops were involved with training Royal Thai Army and Border Police units until departing in September. To commemorate the centennials of two 1860s Maori War units, the Forest Rangers and Taranaki Bush Rangers, the NZSAS Squadron was redesignated 1st Ranger Sdn., NZSAS in January 1963. Between February 1965 and November 1966, 1 to 4 Dets. were rotated to Brunei during the Borneo confrontation.

At first all parachute training was conducted in Australia, with the exception of the first NZ Squadron which received its jump training in Singapore in 1955. A jump school was finally opened at the Royal New Zealand Air Force Base Whenuapai in 1965. The basic jump course lasted four weeks, with at least eight jumps required to graduate. NZSAS selection and training, paralleling that of the ASAS, was followed by six months of specialist training. Interestingly, a significant number of the NZSAS are Maoris.

New Zealand's military assistance to Vietnam began in 1964 when small army elements were deployed to provide civic action support, although some limited material assistance had been given to the French as early as 1952. In 1966 the New Zealand Army Chief of Staff, while visiting the US Military Assistance Command Vietnam, expressed an interest in committing 1st Ranger Sqn., then in Malaysia with 28 Commonwealth Brigade. An alternative proposal was to rotate the squadron's five troops on six-month tours. The deployment of the NZSAS as a whole was particularly desirable to the US command, as there was a pressing need for additional LRRP units. In October 1968 the 26-man 4 Troop, NZSAS was sent to Vietnam via Malaysia where it conducted some preparatory training.

Arriving in Vietnam, 4 Troop was attached to 2 ASAS Sdn. on 12 December. The NZSAS patrol leaders and seconds-in-command initially participated in ASAS patrols to learn the job better before conducting their own missions. Thereafter the NZSAS troop was attached to the resident ASAS squadron as its fourth troop, participating in many combined operations. The Kiwis also adopted the five-man patrol and, unlike the ASAS, retained it after their Vietnam service. Two more troops, also designated 4 Troop, followed for 12-month tours, rotating each November until withdrawn in early February 1971. One sergeant was lost and eight troopers wounded during the 155 missions the NZSAS executed over its 27 months in Vietnam.

Royal Thai Army 1st LRRP Troop
Thailand's involvement in Vietnam was principally a unilateral effort, though with substantial material support from the US. Its efforts were, unlike some allied participation, largely motivated by basic self-interest: i.e., to stop Communist aggression before it further overflowed into Thailand. The first Royal Thai Army (RTA) unit to deploy to Vietnam was the RTA Volunteer Regt., the 'Queen's Cobras', in September 1967. Royal Thai Air Force elements had been present since late 1964, followed by the activation of the Royal Thai Military Assistance Group, Vietnam in early 1966. The 'Queen's Cobras' departed in August 1968, just after their replacement arrived.

The 11,266-man RTA Expeditionary Division, more commonly known as the 'Black Panther' Divisoin, deployed its first increment in late July 1968, accompanied by the 1st LRRP Troop. The second increment arrived in January and February 1969. During the initial planning stages for the development of the Division it had been decided that an LRRP asset was necessary: the 1st LRRP Troop (a reduced company-sized unit) provided this capability. Most of its personnel were transferred from the larger RTA 'Tiger Scout' Recon. Co. based at Ft. Narai, Lopburi, Thailand, co-located with the RTA Special Warfare Center. These organisations were advised and trained by the US 46th Special Forces Company. It is thought that some of its personnel, especially officers and senior NCOs, were detached from the RTA 1st Special Forces Gp., also based at Ft. Narai. As with all RTA units sent to Vietnam, the troops were volunteers of extremely high quality. All were airborne trained (though the unit never made a jump in Vietnam) and Ranger qualified, both being a prerequisite for undertaking Thai Special Forces training.

The 86-man 1st LRRP Troop was actually subordinate to the 1st Armd. Cav. Sdn., a 660-man battalion-sized unit with

a 166-man headquarters and headquarters troop and three 136-man APC-mounted armoured cavalry troops, in addition to the LRRP Troop. The LRRP Troop was organised into a headquarters and two patrol platoons. The US had recommended two LRRP troops, but the Thais preferred additional armoured cavalry strength.

The Division was based at Bearcat in III CTZ's Bien Hoa Province, 30 kilometres east of Saigon, to defend the city's eastern approaches. The Thais proved to be highly professional soldiers who executed well-planned and co-ordinated operations and the soldiers were resourceful and determined. The 1st LRRP Troop conducted reconnaissance and security patrols throughout the Division's TAOR, demonstrating a special ability to detect enemy infiltration attempts in the base camp's vicinity. The Troop did experience some planning and support problems with their parent armoured cavalry squadron because of the armour officers' inexperience with LRRP operations. A number of the Troop's men received additional training at the Military Assistance Command Vietnam Recondo School, operated by the 5th SFGA at Nha Trang.

With the pull-out of other Free World Military Assistance Forces and the further withdrawal of US units, the Thai government announced the incremental reduction of its Vietnam forces in March 1971. The 'Black Panther' Div. began withdrawing elements in July, with the 1st LRRP Troop departing in August. Remaining Division elements were redesignated the RTA Volunteer Force, a reinforced brigade, that same month. This force was withdrawn in March 1972. The 1st LRRP Troop had suffered extremely light losses. It received no unit awards, but the 'Black Panther' Div. as a whole was awarded the US Meritorious Unit Citation along with Vietnamese unit awards.

A USSF NCO checks the sight on a IV Corps MIKE Force M60 near Nui Coto Mountain, 1969. The loader is wearing the Vietnamese jumpwings, and the old MIKE Force patch on his pocket. (Green Beret Magazine)

Troops of the 5th MIKE Force patrol ouside Nha Trang, 1969. The USSF NCO at right is using an AN/PRC-25 radio; the 5th MIKE Force patch can be seen on the pocket of the USSF NCO to the left. (Green Beret Magazine)

NVA 305th Airborne Brigade

The NVA, or more accurately, the Peoples' Army of Vietnam (PAVN), formed its first airborne unit in 1959[1]. Thought to be battalion-sized, but of unknown designation, it was trained and equipped by Chinese Air Force advisors[2]. Its first employment was a combat jump near Muong Soui on the Laotian Plain of Jars on 30 December 1960. This operation helped the Communist Pathet Lao and Neutralist forces in securing the strategic plains. Though not confirmed, another jump was reported the following month north of Vientiane, the Laotian capital.

In 1962 the battalion provided the cadre for the new 305th Airborne Brigade. This 1,400-man unit often conducted training jumps at night to prevent attack by US aircraft. The North Vietnamese airlift capability was limited to a small number of Soviet-built An-2, IL-2 and IL-14 transports, but the unit was capable of dropping crew-served infantry weapons. Its principal rôle was to act as an internal reaction force in the event of invasion from South Vietnam, and to

spearhead a planned future strike into the south. Being based near Hanoi, Brigade elements were used to search for downed US airmen and possible infiltrated special operations teams. The 305th did not execute any combat operations outside North Vietnam, nor is it thought to have made any combat jumps during the course of its internal security operations.

When it became apparent that there would be little immediate need for an airborne force, the brigade was disbanded in March 1967 and its assets used to form the 305th Sapper Command. The Sappers (Dac Cong), a separate PAVN branch, were formally established on 19 March 1967, though provisional sapper units had first been formed during the war with France. The first official units were apparently formed as early as 1957 under the infantry branch. Their mission was the execution of specialised commando-type infiltration, strike, and reconnaissance missions. No other airborne units were formed within the PAVN, until mid-1978 when the 305th Abn. Bde. was reactivated with Soviet assistance.

The Plates

A1: PFC, 1st Brigade, 101st Airborne Division, 1965
When the first US Army units arrived in Vietnam they were outfitted with the OG 107 fatigue uniform worn in the States. Some units had to wait months before tropical uniforms ('jungle fatigues') were issued. The same applied to the

---

[1] Conflicting dates in the history of the PAVN airborne are reported by various reference sources. The years given in this section were chosen as they best fit the sequence of known related events.

[2] The Chinese airborne forces are under Air Force command.

standard leather combat boots and white undershirts. Full-colour insignia were still in use, as were the full-sized sleeve rank insignia. The 101st Recondo patch is worn on the pocket signifying completion of the Division's course at Ft. Campbell. Standard M1956 load-carrying equipment is in use, with a grenade launcher combination tool pouch attached to a universal ammunition pouch, which could hold three 40mm GL rounds[1]. Additional rounds are carried in the bandolier. The M79 GL was one of the most effective weapons employed by infantrymen. The paratrooper depicted in plates A1, A2 and A3 is the same career soldier during three separate Vietnam tours.

A2: Sergeant, 3rd Brigade, 82nd Airborne Division, 1968
The olive green 'jungle fatigues' were by far the most commonly worn and popular uniform in Vietnam. In late 1968 the Army authorised subdued insignia, though some was already in use in Vietnam. Since the issue of such insignia was piecemeal, troops were initially authorised to wear mixed full-colour and subdued insignia. The name and US ARMY

tapes are correctly worn angled with the chest pocket tops. The 82nd Recondo patch is worn on the pocket. Tropical combat boots ('jungle boots') and OG undershirts were also issued to troops in Vietnam. Special ammunition pouches were issued for the M16 rifle since the universal pouch was too deep. The nylon rucksack with frame came into extensive use.

A3: Staff Sergeant, 173rd Airborne Brigade. 1971
Subdued metal pin-on collar rank insignia were authorised in late 1968 and soon replaced the short-lived subdued sleeve rank insignia. In late 1969 it was directed that the name and US Army tapes be worn horizontally, though this was not always complied with. Jungle boots had an improved sole; and a limited issue of nylon M1967 load-carrying equipment was made to some units in 1968, though the cotton M1956 gear remained in general use. An improved tropical rucksack was issued in 1967. The rifle is an M16A1.

The officers and NCOs of USSF Det. A-204, 4th Bn., II Corps MIKE Force pose after returning from a 21-day operation in late 1969. All wear tiger-stripes and all but one are armed with XM177E2 SMGs. (Jess Smetherman)

[1] For additional information on combat equipment, see MAA 205, *U.S. Army Combat Equipments 1910–1988*.

B: Ambush: 173rd Airborne Brigade, 1971
A fire team prepares an ambush kill zone in the An Lao Valley. The grenadier (B1) secures a flank while the team leader (B2) emplaces an M18A1 Claymore mine. The machine gunner (B3), armed with an M60, secures the other flank, while the squad leader (B4) supervises the operation. There were two five-man fire teams in a rifle squad, plus a squad leader. In Vietnam it was not uncommon for squads to have only six or seven men. Some understrength platoons simply combined their three rifle and single weapons squads (with two M60 machine guns) into two squads.

C: ARVN Airborne Division, Hue, Tet-68
The battle for Hue was one of the most brutal fights during the vicious Tet-68 offensive. Though the ARVN Airborne had traditionally worn camouflage uniforms, the battalions committed to Hue wore standard ARVN OG field uniforms. Most of the troops were issued M69 armour vests. Here, an assault team rushes a VC strongpoint: the rifleman (C1) carries a standard ARVN rucksack; a machine gunner (C2), wearing a rain jacket locally made from poncho material (this was a common ARVN practice, and styles varied),

covers the team with an M1919A6 light MG. The platoon leader (C3), a lieutenant, is wearing the US M65 field jacket and is armed with an M1911A1 .45 calibre pistol.

D1: Scout, 1st Force Recon. Company, 1965
Force Recon. Marines initially wore standard OG 107 utilities (Marines do not use the Army term 'fatigues') and the World War II pattern camouflage uniform; tropical utilities were issued in 1966. The headgear is constructed from a steel helmet camouflage cover rigged over a utility cap—not a very common practice. Marine web gear during this period was a mix of World War II era items—M1910 canteen carrier and M1943 suspenders, first aid pouch, three-pocket grenade pouch, sub-machine gun magazine pouch, and light marching pack—coupled with the M1961 rifle belt designed for the Marines' unique M14 rifle ammunition pouches. When the 1st Force Recon. Co. arrived in Vietnam they were armed with the M3A1 'grease gun' SMG, found to be ill-suited for the more aggressive combat patrols they were forced to conduct. In early 1965 they traded the USSF two rubber assault boats for 200 M2 carbines. Later M16A1 rifles were issued to all Marine units.

D2: Patrol Leader, 3rd Force Recon. Company, 1971
The camouflage jungle utilities were adopted as the standard field uniform in 1968. Due to piecemeal issue, OG and camouflage items could be mixed during the first year of

A group of II Corps MIKE Force NCOs, wearing the 2nd MIKE Force Command pocket patch, celebrate a victory in their club during 1969. The unit banner is principally white on black. (Pete Lopez)

issue. Most Marine web items had been replaced by the Army's M1956 equipment, though Marines were still universally issued the jungle first aid kit. The nylon rucksack with frame, plus the smaller tropical rucksack, were also issued. The inset insignia is an unofficial Force Recon. badge; Force Recon. Marines seldom, if ever, wore any form of insignia in the field. Though unrelated to this figure, Force Recon. Marines tended to wear various styles of football helmets when conducting parachute jumps.

D3: Pathfinder, 25th Aviation Battalion, 1969

Camouflage tropical uniform was authorised for Ranger/ LRRP, Pathfinder, and scout and tracker dog units, though they were also issued OG jungle fatigues. The Pathfinder patch, in use since World War II, was usually worn on the left chest pocket of field uniforms; on the Class A Army Green coat the patch was worn centred on the left forearm. His 'dog tags' are attached to his bootlaces, a common Vietnam practice. This Pathfinder's equipment consists of an AN/ PRC-25 radio with a special headset permitting free use of the hands and a Model 193-001 visible approach path indicator. The VAPI projects a very narrow beam of light which can only be seen by pilots if on a direct line of sight. The Pathfinder will 'talk' a pilot into position so that he can see the light before making his approach into a restricted landing zone, enabling him to avoid vertical obstructions. He is armed with an XM177E2 sub-machine gun.

2 Sdn., ASAS fighting patrol preparing for helicopter insertion in 1971. A wide variety of equipment and weapons can be seen. The two men in the foreground have an M16A1 mounting an M203 grenade launcher and an M60 MG. (ASAS)

D4: Pathfinder, 1st Aviation Battalion, 1970

Since the late 1950s the Pathfinders have worn black 'baseball' caps with various insignia. Besides the Pathfinder patch, jumpwings (sometimes backed by the unit coloured oval) were worn, with or without small brass rank insignia. Besides unofficial Pathfinder scrolls and tabs identifying their units, officially they wore an airborne tab over their parent formation's shoulder patch. The 1st Inf. Div., the 'Big Red One', defied regulations and refused to wear the black '1' of a subdued patch.

E1: Dai Uy, ARVN Special Forces, 1970

The LLDB wore a dark green beret in French style with the embroidered LLDB badge on the right side. The LLDB, like most special ARVN formations, had their own camouflage uniform; this captain's version is cut along the lines of the US jungle fatigues. Like their USSF counterparts, the LLDB received honorary presentation of their counterpart's jumpwings. The early (inset) shoulder patch was used from 1959 to 1963. The early metal beret badge (inset), used prior to 1963, came in two size variations, 30mm and 45mm.

E2: Ha Si, 91st Airborne Ranger Battalion 1967
The 91st (later 81st) Ranger Battalion, unlike other Ranger Command units, was under the direct control of the LLDB. For this reason the battalion wore the LLDB patch and dark green beret, rather than the Ranger Command patch and red beret. The unit also wore the standard LLDB camouflage fatigues. This *Biet Cach* sergeant is armed with an M79GL.

E3: Striker, 5th MIKE Force, 1967
A tiger-stripe beret was authorised for MIKE Forces, though it was not widely worn; Montagnard Strikers seemed to favour it more than other ethnic groups, however. A MIKE Force beret flash was also authorised, though more often than not no insignia were worn on the beret. In rare instances the flash was even worn as a shoulder patch. World War II web gear was common, but M1956 equipment was also in wide use, often mixed with earlier gear. An M1918A2 Bar was authorised for each MIKE Force squad, though these were withdrawn when M16A1 rifles were issued in 1969.

F1: Rifleman, ARVN Airborne Group, 1955
At this early date the new ARVN forces still used French uniforms and equipment along with US web gear. US weapons were coming into more common usage, but French weapons were still issued to some units. This young para-trooper, committed against opposition militant groups in Saigon, is armed with a French 7.5mm MAS 1936 rifle.

F2: Trung Si, ARVN Airborne Brigade, 1963
This sergeant is outfitted in the early ARVN airborne camouflage uniform adopted in the late 1950s. Its pattern and cut were influenced by similar British uniforms issued to the French Union forces in Indochina[1]. A jump designator badge, indicating the individual as being assigned to a unit on jump status, is worn on the left pocket. His weapon is an M1A1 carbine, and his web gear a mix of World War II and M1956 items.

F3: Trung Uy, ARVN Airborne Division, 1972
This first lieutenant is uniformed in the late model ARVN camouflage adopted in the late 1960s. The early pattern camouflage was still sometimes worn by senior officers. On his pattern-painted helmet he has painted his US equivalent rank. It was popular among the Vietnamese to have various styles of combat vests and rain jacket made at personal expense.

F4: Paratrooper, ARVN Airborne Division
The red French-style para beret was worn by the ARVN Airborne with an embroidered badge on the right side. This paratrooper is equipped with a US-made T-7A parachute.

G1: Patrol Commander, ASAS
The US camouflage jungle fatigues were the most common 'ops' uniform used by the Australian SAS, and have since been adopted as their standard field uniform. Wide leeway was permitted in both uniforms and headgear. This NCO is armed with a Stirling L34A1 silenced SMG. His equipment is a mix of British-style '58 and '44 pattern items. US M1956 web gear was also used, mixed with their own. Other Patrol

weapons included the commonly used M16A1 rifle, XM177E2 SMG, little-used FN L1A1 rifle (too heavy), and M60 machine gun (on ambushes).

G2: Patrol Second-in-Command, ASAS
The headband appears to have been in wide use by the ASAS, though many of the troops went bareheaded. Besides US camouflage and OG jungle fatigues, the ASAS also made limited use of tiger stripes, but seldom wore their own OG tropical uniform in the field. US fragmentation and smoke grenades were standard issue. Extensive use was made of the M79, XM148 (pictured), and M203 grenade launchers, with

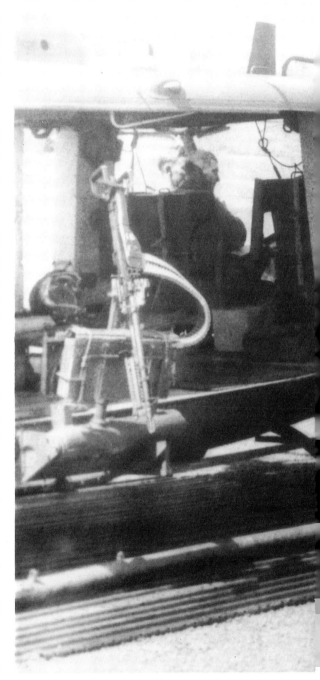

[1] See An ARVN Paratrooper Uniform, 1965–66, *Military Illustrated Past & Present* No. 11, Feb.–March 1988.

one or two being carried by each Patrol. It was a common practice to dab weapons with camouflaging paint.

G3: Signaller, ASAS
The ASAS, unlike US LRRP and reconnaissance units, commonly used camouflage paint. The camouflage beret was another popular headgear item. The Australians began the practice of protecting machine gun belts with rubber tubes cut from US-issue inflatable sleeping pads (air mattresses); later a purpose-made belt protector was adopted. Though they were seldom used, the ASAS had modified FN L1A1 rifles by cutting down the barrel, gas piston tube, and forearm, plus other modifications. Due to its excessive muzzle blast and recoil, it was aptly known as 'The Bitch'.

G4: Medic, ASAS
Wearing the summer shirt, this trooper displays his SAS jumpwings on the right shoulder. The ASAS had worn a maroon beret until adopting the British-style sand-colour in

A patrol of 3 Sdn., ASAS prepares to board a 9 Helicopter Sdn. UH-1B in 1969. They wear US camouflage jungle fatigues, and have water bladders under the jackets. Three are armed with FN L1A1 rifles and two with M16s; the man to the right has an XM148 grenade launcher fitted on his M16. (ASAS)

1964 when 1 SAS Regt. was formed. The ASAS beret badge is identical to the British. Though the ASAS are authorised to wear an 'SAS' shoulder strap title, all units deployed to Vietnam used a common 'AUSTRALIA' title. The blue shoulder lanyard also signified the individual's SAS assignment.

G5: Troop Commander, NZSAS
In the field New Zealand SAS troops were indistinguishable from the Australians. However, service uniforms were distinctly different. The NZSAS retained the maroon 'cherry' beret until 1986. The shoulder title was worn only on uniform coats, and has since been replaced by a different version.

H1: Sergeant, 1st LRRP Troop, Royal Thai 'Black Panther' Division
This NCO is undertaking helicopter rappelling training at the MACV Recondo School, operated by the 5th Special Forces Group. Thai forces used almost exclusively US equipment and uniforms, but did have some unique uniform items. The tiger stripes used by the Thai Special Forces and Rangers had a higher percentage of black than other versions. The back beret was also used by Thai Ranger units. The insert insigmia is the shoulder patch (sometimes worn on chest pockets) of the Royal Thai 'Black Panther' Division.

H2, H3, Corporal, 350th NVA Airborne Brigade
The NVA airborne brigade was equipped by the Communist Chinese and used the same summer jump uniform and related items. This, in turn, was influenced by similar Soviet items. The parachute is a copy of the Soviet D-5 coupled with an older model chest-mounted reserve. Collar rank insignia were commonly worn in North Vietnam, but seldom used by NVA troops in the South. His weapon is the folding-stock version of the AK-47 assault rifle, generally strapped to the top of the reserve when jumping. There has been much speculation as to the design of NVA jumpwings with no confirmed designs being known. It is thought that they were similar to the Soviet parachutist badge.

I: Jumpwings
A wide variety of designs, materials, and constructions will be found for all countries' jumpwings. US and Thai wings were worn on the left chest, Vietnamese on the right chest, and Australian and New Zealand on the right upper sleeve.
I1: US Basic Parachutist Badge. It is depicted on an 82nd Abn. Div. oval (officially, 'airborne background trimming'). Battalions and some companies had their own ovals.
I2: US Senior Parachutist Badge. Worn on 101st Abn. Div. oval.
I3: US Master Parachutist Badge. Worn on a 173rd Abn. Bde. oval.
I4: US Rigger Badge. This embroidered badge was worn unofficially on the left chest by parachute riggers.
I5: US Marine Corps Parachutist Badge. Marines were trained at the Army Airborne Course and initially awarded the Army's basic badge (I1). After completing jumps with their Marine

A camouflage-painted 2 Sdn. ASAS Patrol prepares for take-off on a UH-1B in 1971. The foreground man has an M203 grenade launcher, and the one behind him an XM148 GL, both mounted on M16s. The man to the left has an FN L1A1 rifle. (ASAS)

Unit they are awarded the gold Marine wings (also used by the Navy).

I6: Vietnamese Honorary Basic Parachutist Badge. While similar to the standard Vietnamese jumpwings, this version was presented to US personnel who jumped with ARVN units and MIKE Force CIDG. All USSF personnel and ARVN Airborne advisors were also honorarily authorised to wear these wings, even though they may never have jumped with the LLDB. Senior and master versions, with the same devices as I8 and I9, also existed. Many US personnel wore standard Vietnamese wings, being unaware that there was a difference.

I7: Vietnamese Basic Parachutist Badge. The star represented the North Star, a Vietnamese symbol for truth and guidance.

I8: Vietnamese Senior Parachutist Badge. This was a common embroidered version.

I9: Vietnamese Master Parachutist Badge. Another common embroidered version.

I10: Vietnamese Basic Monitor Badge. The monitor, or instructor, rating was seldon awarded; it required extensive experience and a broad range of skills, including a large number of freefall jumps. Monitors assigned to the ARVN Abn. Bde./ Div. wore a maroon felt backing.

I11: Vietnamese Senior Monitor Badge. Some monitor badges were embroidered in white, but this was only an unauthorised variation.

I12: Vietnamese Master Monitor Badge. The interlocking yellow and red rings represented the national colours, but some versions had different colour rings for no known reason.

I13: Australian SAS Parachute Brevet. This version was intended for wear on service coats, but in Vietnam was worn on OG tropical shirts and summer shirts.

I14: Royal Thai Basic Parachutist Badge. A large number of attractive Thai wing variations and styles will be encountered.

I15: New Zealand SAS Parachute Brevet. Both Australian and New Zealand SAS wings were influenced by their British counterparts.

J: ARVN Airborne Shoulder Patches
Vietnamese patches were either printed on thin cloth or finely embroidered in silk-like thread, similar to the German

ASAS soldiers outside the dining hall at Nui Dat prepare to depart on an operation. Though difficult to see, the foreground man (back to camera), and the fourth man form the left, have silenced L34A1 SMGs with the stocks removed. (ASAS)

'Bevo' style. Subdued versions were sometimes used. All were worn on the left shoulder.

J1: ARVN Airborne Group. Used from 1955 to December 1959. The ARVN Airborne patches were heavily influenced by the French.

J2: ARVN Airborne Brigade. Used from 1959 to December 1965.

J3: ARVN Airborne Division. Used from 1965 to 1975.

J4: ARVN Special Forces. Used from 1963 to the end of 1970. A redesign of the earlier LLDB patch (see E1 inset). The three lightning bolts had the same meaning as those on the USSF patch: sea, air, and land infiltration.

J5: 81st Airborne Ranger Battalion. This is one of many, and widely different, unofficial patches used by the 91st/81st Rangers. Officially they wore the LLDB patch (J4).

J6: Special Exploitation Service. Worn by Vietnamese personnel of their MACV-SOG counterpart organisation.

K: US Army Airborne Patches and Crests
Unit patches (officially, 'shoulder sleeve insignia'—SSI) were worn on the left shoulder. A soldier's former combat unit's SSI could be worn on the right shoulder. Subdued SSIs were black and OD. Crests (officially, 'distinctive unit insignia'—DI) were worn on Army Green, Army Tan, and Army Khaki uniforms shoulder straps by all ranks. Airborne troops did not wear it on the Army Green garrison cap like other troops, but rather wore the 'glider patch' described elsewhere in this book. The DIs pictured here were worn by division and separate brigade HHCs (divisional brigade HHCs wore the division's), and companies and detachments not assigned to battalions. All battalions had their own DI.

K1: 3rd Brigade, 82nd Airborne Division SSI. The 'AA' and colours represent 'All Americans', the Division's official nickname.

K2: 3rd Brigade, 82nd Airborne Division DI. The fleur-de-lys symbolises the Division's World War I honours. The wings are symbolic of the Division's airborne mission. Also worn by the Division HHC and other brigade HHCs.

K3: 101st Airborne Division SSI. The black shield represents the Civil War 'Iron Brigade', and the eagle one of the Iron Brigade's regimental mascots.

K4: 101st Airborne Division DI. The diving eagle alludes to the Division's airborne rôle.

K5: 1st Brigade (Airborne), 1st Cavalry Division (Airmobile) SSI. Though authorised for all the Division's airborne elements, the airborne tab was not always worn.

K6: 1st Brigade (Airborne), 1st Cavalry Division (Airmobile) DI. Also worn by the Division HHC and other brigade HHCs.

K7: 173rd Airborne Brigade (Separate) SSI. The bayonet represents the Brigade's paratroopers, and the wing the method by which it deployed to combat.

K8: 173rd Airborne Brigade (Separate) DI. The stylised wing and parachute allude to the Brigade's airborne mission. The sword represents the 1967 combat jump.

K9: Airborne Advisory Team 162 SSI. Worn by ARVN Airborne Division advisors. This was the Military Assistance Command, Vietnam SSI. In the field the advisors wore the ARVN Airborne Division patch (J3).

L: Airborne Equipment. A wide variety of airborne equipment was used by US forces. The most commonly used items are described here.

L1: T-10 Main Parachute. Adopted in 1952 to replace the T-

The 'Glider Patch' (officially, 'airborne insignia') was worn on the Army Green garrison cap in place of the unit crest worn by non-airborne personnel. White parachute and glider, red border, medium blue backing, $2\frac{1}{4}$ in. in diameter: (L) officers, (R) enlisted men. (US Army)

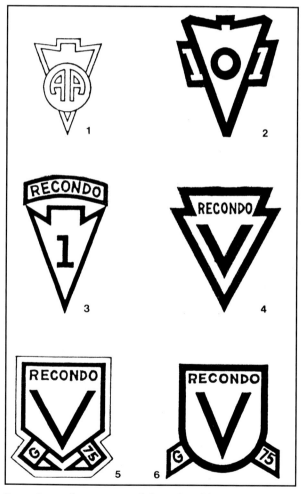

Recondo patches, worn on left pocket: (1) 82nd Abn. Div.—red-bordered white arrowhead and 'AA', medium blue disc. (2) 101st Abn. Div.—black and white as pictured; (3) 1st Cavalry Div. (Airmobile)—white portions are OD, black as pictured; (4) Military Assistance Command Vietnam—black and white as pictured; (5) Co. G (Ranger), 75th Inf.—white portions are OD, black as pictured; (6) Co. G (Ranger), 75th Inf. (variation)—same colours as (5). (Drawn by LTC Ronald L. Kirshman)

Various Mobile Strike Force shoulder patches, usually worn on left shoulder: (top, L to R) MIKE Forces, 1965–67—white on black; 1st and 2nd MIKE Forces, 1967–70—gold on black tab, medium blue shield, black and white knife, red crossbow, gold lighting, bow string and border; 3rd, 4th and 5th MIKE Forces, 1967–70—gold on black tab, medium blue shield, black and white knife, yellow lighting, black border. (Bottom) 2nd MIKE Force Command (USSF only on left pocket), 1968–70—gold on black tab, white backing with gold details and border, dark green dragon with gold details, red flame, gold and red Vietnamese flag stripes; (bottom R) Official MIKE Forces (the others were semi-official, but usually retained), 1968–70—green shield, black parachute with white details, natural-colour tiger's head, white border.

7A, it used a 35-foot olive green parabolic canopy. A 15-foot static line deployed the parachute. The nylon harness had a single-point chest release. The long waist strap to the side is for attaching the reserve, which also snaps to D-rings on the harness.

L2: T-10R Reserve Parachute. The chest-mounted reserve used a 24-foot white, flat, circular canopy in a cotton canvas container. It was deployed by a side-mounted ripcord handle.

L3: M1950 Adjustable Individual Weapons Case. Designed to carry small arms (M16 rifle, M60 MG, M79 GL), its length could be adjusted by folding any excess bottom end behind itself and securing with a strap and buckle. Lined with thick felt padding, it was intended to protect both jumper and

weapon. It was swapped to the reserve D-ring on the left side. If jumping a machine gun, it was dropped (at about 200 feet) on a 15-foot lowering line prior to landing, further protecting the jumper from injury. It was not uncommon to jump with weapons exposed, in which case they were strapped muzzle down (after taping on padding) under the reserve's waist band.

L4: Weapons and Individual Equipment Container. The WIEC (pronounced 'wick') could carry up to 95 lbs. of weapons, ammunition, and unit equipment, such as radios. It was attached under the jumper's reserve to the harness D-rings and dropped on an 18-foot lowering line prior to landing. Its size was adjustable by the use of straps and buckles. This item was burdensome to jump, and those so 'honoured' were the first in the door due to the difficulty of moving in a pitching aircraft with such a load.

L5: Kit Bag and H-harness. While individual web gear could be worn under the parachute harness, it was often jumped, along with small items of unit equipment, in an aviator's kit bag. Bundled in an H-harness strap system, it was snapped to the parachute harness D-rings. The H-harness was also used to jump rucksacks in the same manner. Kit bags with more than 35lbs. and rucksacks with frames were dropped on a 15-foot lowering line. All paratroopers jumped with a kit bag, folded under the reserve if not used to carry equipment. The main canopy, pack tray, and harness were packed into it after landing, and the reserve was snapped to the bag's web carrying handles.

Notes sur les planches en couteur

A1 Uniformes tropics, tee-shirts verts et insignes adoucis n'avaient pas encore été distribués. L'insigne sur la poche signifie qu'il a passé le cours de reconnaisance de sa division. **A2** Le même soldat; une période de service plus tard au Vietnam. L'uniforme de jungle est maintenant en usage, quoiqu'une mélange d'insignies adoucis et en plein couleurs était toujours fréquente. L'insigne du cours de reconnaissance de la 82nd est porté sur la poche. Des nouvelles cartouchières ont été distribuées pour l'équipement de 1956; aussi un sac à dos avec armature. **A3** Ces insignes de grade en métal sombre sont portés maintenant sur le col. Les rubans de nom et *US Army* étaient officiellement portés horizontalement sur la poitrine à partir de la fin de 1969. Quelques ceinturons à sangles de 1967 ont été distribués, et il existait un sac à dos amélioré.

B1 Le grenadier garde le flanc pendant que le commandant de l'équipe (**B2**) pose une mine *Claymore*. L'autre flanc est gardé par le mitrailleur (**B3**); le commandant du groupe (**B4**) dirige la préparation de l'embuscade.

C Les parachutistes ARVN à Hue portaient des uniformes verts plutôt que les uniformes de camouflage normaux, et la plupart d'entre eux avaient des gilets pare-balles M69. Le fusilier (**C1**) a le sac à dos ordinaire ARVN. Le mitrailleur (**C2**), qui porte un M1919A6, a une veste imperméable fabriquée sur place en étoffe de poncho. Le lieutenant (**C3**) porte la veste US M65.

D1 Les marines de reconnaissance portaient au début une mélange de tenue de corvée OG107 et vêtements de camouflage de la deuxième guerre mondiale. La couverture de casque est porté ici par-dessus un calot de camouflage. Au ceinturon M1961, destiné aux chargeurs M14, il y a attaché de l'équipement de la deuxième guerre mondiale. La mitraillette M3 était remplacée plus tard par la carabine M2 et le fusil M16. **D2** Les uniformes de camouflage étaient d'usage courant à partir de 1968, et les ceinturons à sangles de l'armée M1956 avaient en la plupart déjà supplanté ceux des marines. L'insigne du *Marine Force Recon* dans le schéma en cartouche n'était pas officiel. **D3** L'insigne *Pathfinder* est porté sur la pouche gauche. Le poste de radio AN/PRC 25 cst utilisé conjointement avec le projecteur M193–001 qui guide le pilote vers le terrain d'atterrissage. Il porte la mitraillette XM177E2. **D4** Les *Pathfinders* portaient une casquette de base-ball noire avec l'insigne *Pathfinder*, les insignes de parachutiste en forme des ailes, et quelquefois des signes de grade en cuivre. Ils portaient des titres *Airborne* sur les épaules, au-dessus de l'insigne de l'unité mère.

E1 Le béret, l'insigne et l'uniforme de camouflage étaient particulier au LLDB. Les insignes dans le schéma en cartouche sont ceux qu'on trouve sur l'épaule et sur le béret avant 1963. **E2** Cette unité était sous le commandement du LLDB et ils portaient l'uniforme et les insignes du LLDB. **E3** Le béret et parement à raie de tigre étaient autorisés, mais pas universellement portés par les soldats du *MIKE Force*. Une mélange de ceinturons à sangles de 1956 et de la deuxième guerre mondiale était normale. Le *BAR* était distribué à toutes escouades avant la distribution du M16 en 1969.

F1 Uniformes français, ceinturons à sangles des Etats Unis, et une mélange d'armes françaises et des Etats Unis étaient normaux à cette date. **F2** Une copie de l'étoffe de camouflage britannique utilisée par les parachutistes français, était adoptée par les parachutistes ARVN dans les années cinquante. L'insigne sur la poche marque adhésion à une unité de parachutistes en campagne. **F3** L'uniforme de camouflage ARVN adopté vers la fin des années soixante. Les divers vestes imperméables et gilets de treillis étaient personnellement acquis. **F4** Le béret de style français était retenu par le *ARVN Airborne*. Le parachute est un US T-7A.

G1 Uniforme de camouflage des Etats Unis était le plus fréquent parmi les troupes SAS australiennes. Les ceinturons à sangles sont une mélange des dessins britanniques de 1944 et 1958; l'arme est la mitraillette *Stirling* avec silencieux. **G2** Uniformes verts et à raie de tigre des Etats Unis étaient aussi en usage, et un grand nombre d'armes et de grenades étant porté. **G3** Le béret de camouflage et le fard de camouflage étaient populaires parmi les ASAS. La cartouchière de la mitrailleuse est protégée par des tubes plastiques coupés d'un matelas pneumatique. Le fusil à canon scié L1A1 n'était pas populaire, et était surnommé "la garce". **G4** Remarquez les ailes de parachutiste SAS sur l'épaule droite, le titre *Australia* sur les épaules, porte' à la place des titres d'unité au Vietnam, et le béret et cordon régimentaire. **G5** Le NZSAS retenait le béret bordeaux jusqu'à 1986.

H1 Béret noir et camouflage à raie de tigre foncé étaient typiques des *Thai Rangers*, qui portaient autrement des vêtements et de l'équipement pour la plupart américains. **H2**, **H3** Uniforme communiste chinois, et des copies du parachute soviétique D–5 avec un sac de réserve ventral; les signes de grade sur le col n'étaient portés qu'au Vietnam du Nord.

I Il existe beaucoup de variations de dessin, couleur et matériaux parmi les ailes de parachutiste de toutes nations. Celles des Etats Unis et de la Thaïlande étaient portées à gauche sur la poitrine, celles du Vietnam à droite, et celles de l'Australie et de la Nouvelle-Zélande sur le bras droite. Pour identification, voir les légendes en anglais.

J Les insignes d'épaule *ARVN Airborne* étaient imprimés ou brodés et étaient portés sur l'épaule gauche. Pour identification, voir les légendes en anglais.

K Les insignes d'épaule d'unité étaient portés à la gauche. Les cimiers (insignes distinctifs) étaient portés sur les bretelles des uniformes de campagne et des habits d'ordonnance. Pour identification, voir les légendes en anglais.

Farbthfeln

A1 Tropenuniformen, grüne T-Shirts und gedämpfte Insignien waren noch nicht ausgegeben worden. Die Tascheninsignien bedeuten, daß er die Erkundungskursus der Division bestanden hat. **A2** Derselbe Soldat; eine spätere Dienstzeit in Vietnam. Die Dschungeluniform ist jetzt in Gebrauch, obwohl eine Mischung von gedämpften und vollfarbigen Insignien war noch häufig. Die Insignien der Erkundunskursus des 82nd wird an der Tasche getragen. Neue Patronentaschen sind für das 1956er Gurtband ausgegeben worden, auch ein Rucksack mit Traggestell. **A3** Dunkle Metallinsignien werden jetzt auf dem Kragen getragen. US Army- und Namenbänder wurden von Ende 1969 an offiziell horizontal an der Brust getragen. Manche 1967er Gurtbänder waren ausgegeben worden, und es gab einen verbesserten Rucksack.

B1 Der Grendarier bewacht die Flanke, während der Gruppenführer (**B2**) eine *Claymore* Mine legt. Die andere Flanke wird von dem Soldat mit Maschinengewehr (**B3**) bewacht; der Abteilungsführer (**B4**) überwacht die Vorbereitung der Hinterhalt.

C ARVN Fallschirmjäger in Hue trugen grüne Uniformen statt den gewöhnlichen Tarnzügen, und die meisten davon hatten M69 kugelsichere Westen. Der Gewehrschütze (**C1**) hat den ARVN Standardrucksack. Der Soldat mit Maschinengewehr (**C2**), der ein M1919A6 trägt, hat eine am Ort aus Ponchostoff gemachte Regenjacke. Der Leutnant (**C3**), trägt die Jacke US M65.

D1 Anfangs trugen Aufklärungsmarinetruppen eine Mischung von OG107 Arbeitsanzügen und Tarnzügen vom zweiten Weltkrieg. Die Helmdecke ist hier über einer Arbeitskappe getragen. Am Patronengurt M1961, der für M14 Patronen bestimmt ist, sind verschiedene Ausrüstungstücke befestigt. Die Maschinenpistole M3 wurde später durch den M2 Karabiner und das M16 Gewehr ersetzt. **D2** Tarnuniformen waren ab 1968 im allgemein ausgegeben, und M1956 Armeegurtbänder hatten mittlerweile die Gurtbänder der Marineeinfanterie meistens abgelöst. Die Insignien des *Marine Force Recon* im Nebenbild waren inoffiziell. **D3** Die *Pathfinder* Insignien werden auf der linken Tasche getragen. Der Radioapparat AN/PRC–25 wird in Verbindung mit einem M193-001 Scheinwerfer benutzt, der dem, Pilot den Anflugweg weist. Er trägt die XM177E2 Maschinenpistole. **D4** *Pathfinders* trugen schwarze Baseballkappen mit dem *Pathfinder* Insignien, Fallschirmflügel und manchmal Rangmarke aus Messing. Sie trugen *Airborne* Schultertiteln über den Insignien ihres Stammtruppenteils.

E1 Die Baskenmütze, Plakette und Tarnuniform waren eigentümlich für das LLDB. Die Insignien im Nebenbild sind die Sculterflecken und die Baskenmützeplakette, die vor 1963 benutzt wurden. **E2** Diese Einheit war unter dem Kommando des LLDB, und sie trugen LLDB Uniformen und Insignien. **E3** Die tigerstreifige Baskenmütze und der Flecken waren autorisiert, obwohl nicht allgemein unter *MIKE Force* Soldaten getragen. Eine Mischung von 1956er Gurtband und Gurtband vom zweiten Weltkrieg war normal. Das BAR war allen Korporalschaften ausgebeben, bis der Ausgabe des M16 in 1969.

F1 Französische Uniformen, US Gurtbänder und eine Mischung von US und französischen Gewehren auf dieser Zeit normal. **F2** Eine Kopie des britischen Tarnstoffs, der von französischen Fallschirmjägern benutzt wurde, wurde in den fünfziger Jahren von ARVN Fallschirmjägern angepasst. Die Plakette an der Tasche deutet zur ständigen Verfügung stehenden Fallschirmjägereinheit an. **F3** Die ARVN Tarnuniform, die spät in den sechziger Jahren übergenommen wurde. Verschiedene Regenjacken und Kampfwesten wurden persönlich erworben. **F4** Die Baskenmütze im französischen Stil wurde von dem ARVN *Airborne* behalten. Der Fallschirm is ein US-T-7A.

G1 Die US Tarnuniform war die häufigste Uniform unter australischen SAS Truppen. Gurtbänder waren eine Mischung von britischen 1944er und 1958er Mustern; die Waffe ist die *Stirling* Maschinengewehr mit Schalldämpfer. **G2** US grüne und tigerstreifige Uniformen waren auch in Gebrauch, und eine große Auswahl an US Waffen und Granaten wurde getragen. **G3** Die Tarnbaskenmütze und Tarnfarbe waren unter dem ASAS beliebt. Die Patronentasche ist mit Gummischlauch geschützt, der von Luftmatratzen geschnitten worden ist. Das L1A1 Gewehr mit abgesägtem Lauf war nicht beliebt, und wurde "die Hure" gennant. **G4** Siehe die SAS Fallschirmjägerflügel auf dem rechten Schulter, den Schultertitel, "Australia", in Vietnam statt Einheitstiteln getragen, und Regimentsbaskenmütze und Kordel. **G5** Das NZSAS behielt die kastanienbraune Baskenmütze bis 1986.

H1 Schwarze Baskenmütze und dunkle tigerstreifige Tarnung waren typisch für *Thai Rangers* die sonst meistens amerikanische Kleidung und Ausrüstung benutzten. **H2**, **H3** Kommunistische chinesische Uniformen und Kopien von dem D–5 sowjetischen Fallschirm und Reservegepäck; die Kragenabzeichen wurden nur in Nordvietnam getragen.

I Viele Variationen von Konstruktion, Farbe und Material werden bei den Fallschirmjägern aller Nationen gefunden. US und thailändische Flügel wurden links an der Brust getragen, vietnamesische an der rechten Seite, australische und neuseeländische rechts am Oberarm. Identifizierung im englischen Bildtext.

J ARVN *Airborne* Schulterinsignien wurden entweder gedruckt oder gestrickt, und auf dem linken Schulter getragen. Identifizierung im englischen Bildtext.

K US Einheitsschulteringsignien wurden an der linken Seite getragen.

L1 Ce parachute, adopté en 1952, avait une voilure verte de dix mètres; la ceinture longue est attachée au sac de réserve, qui est à son tour attaché aux anneaux en forme de D du harnais. L2 Celui avait une voilure blanche de sept mètres. L3 Cette boîte protegeait toutes petites armes ordinaires; si la mitrailleuse M60 était portée, elle serait laissée tomber au bout d'une corde de cinq mètres avant la descente. Elle était attaché à l'anneau en forme de D à la gauche. L4 Ce conteneur porte jusqu'à quarante kilos d'armes, munitions et postes de radio, etc. Attaché aux anneaux en forme de D du harnais sous le sac de réserve, il était laissé tomber au bout d'une corde de six mètres avant la descente. L5 De l'équipement était souvent porté dans ce sac, fourni avec un système de sangles en forme de H attaché aux anneaux en forme de D. Le harnais en forme de H était aussi utilisé pour les sacs à dos. Les sacs d'ordonnance qui pésaient plus que seize kilos et les sacs à dos étaient laissés tomber au bout d'une corde de cinq mètres avant la descente.

Helmschmucke (kennzeichende Insignien) wurden auf den Schulterstücken Dienstanzüge unter Straßenuniformen getragen. Identifizierung im englischen Bildtext.

L1 Dieser Fallschirm, in 1952 übernommen, hatte eine zehnmeterlange grüne Fallschirmkappe; der lange Taillenriemen ist an dem Reservegepäck befestigt, das auch an den D-Ringen des Gurtwerks befestigt ist. L2 Dieser Fallschirm hatte eine weiße siebenmeterlange Fallschirmkappe. L3 Dieses Kästchen schützte alle Standardhandfeuerwaffen; wenn das M60 Maschinengewehr getragen würde, dann würde es am Ende einer fünfmeterlangen Linie vor der Landung losgelassen werden. Es wurde an dem D-Ring an der linken Seite befestigt. L4 Dieser Behälter konnte bis zu vierzig Kilos von Gewehren, Radioapparaten und Munition usw, beförden. An den D-Ringen des Gurtwerks unter dem Reservegepäck befestigt, er wurde am Ende einer sechsmeterlangen Linie vor der Landung heruntergelassen. L5 Gurtbänder wurden oft in diesem Sack getragen, der mit einem System in der Form eines "H" betakelt und an den D-Ringen befestigt wurde. Das H-Gurtwerk wurde auch für Rucksäcke benutzt. Säcke die mehr als sechzehn Kilos wogen und Rucksäcke wurden am Ende einer fünfmeterlangen Linie heruntergelassen.